Scented
Gifts

Scented Gifts

from sachets to soaps,
from gingerbread to potpourri

Laura Dover Doran

Lark Books

For Patrick, who endures all my projects with good humor and patience.

Art Direction/Production: Elaine Thompson
Photography: Evan Bracken
Illustrations and Watercolors: Bobby Gold
Editorial Assistance: Evans Carter and Catharine Sutherland
Proofreader: Julie Brown

Library of Congress Cataloging-in-Publication Data
Doran, Laura Dover, 1970–
    Scented gifts : from sachets to soap, from gingerbread to potpourri /
by Laura Dover Doran. -- 1st ed.
      p. cm.
    Includes index.
    ISBN 1-57990-035-6
    1. Handicraft.   2. Potpourris (Scented floral mixtures)   3. Gifts.
TT157.D637   1998
    745.5--dc21   97-45872
                                     CIP

10 9 8 7 6 5 4 3 2 1

First Edition

Published by Lark Books
50 College St.
Asheville, NC 28801, USA

© 1998, Lark Books

Distributed by Random House,Inc., in the United States, Canada,
   the United Kingdom, Europe, and Asia

Distributed in Australia by Capricorn Link (Australia) Pty Ltd.,
   P.O. Box 6651, Baulkham Hills Business Centre, NSW 2153, Australia

Distributed in New Zealand by Tandem Press Ltd.,
   2 Rugby Rd., Birkenhead, Auckland, New Zealand

Printed in Hong Kong

ISBN 1-57990-035-6

Contents

Acknowledgments

First, I would like to extend my heartfelt gratitude to

Mardi and Kellett Letson, who opened their home

to the staff of Lark Books. Thanks also to the

following people for providing photography props:

Kelly Davis, Corky Kurzmann, Georgia Shuford, and Jeff Webb.

Pier 1 Imports and Natural Home, both in Asheville, North Carolina,

were gracious enough to lend a number of items from their shelves.

And finally, many thanks to Evans Carter (who researched, carted, and measured),

Catharine Sutherland (who compiled the chart on page 36),

and Art Director Elaine Thompson, for her design sense,

creative eye, and enthusiasm for the project.

Introduction

In an antique store recently, an unexpected whiff of a wooden dresser transported me back to Pleasant Gardens Elementary. Instantly, I recalled my childhood school, the musty, pine halls in particular—a place that smelled remarkably like that old dresser. It was a spot I hadn't thought of in years, but, in that moment, I remembered it perfectly.

Whether we are conscious of it or not, fragrance can hold powerful associations. Imagine, for example, the holiday season without its familiar aromas: the evergreen, the roaring fire, the cookies in the oven. Scent is an essential part of our experience.

And though scarcely any among us would disagree that our noses are important sensory organs, that seems to be where the agreement ends. Some are drawn to floral scents; others are fond of spicy or citrusy aromas. Some feel the more subtle and delicate the scent, the better. Although all of the projects in this book are scented, the types and degree of the fragrances vary widely. I have tried to provide a gift idea for everyone on your list, regardless of their opinions about scent. And you should feel no guilt about varying the degree of scent to suit your tastes—or those of the recipient.

Which brings me to the second focus of the book: all of the projects are also designed as gifts. I have found that crafters really do find it more satisfying to give than to receive. Handmade gifts are usually less expensive and often take very little time to make. And, of course, don't forget to make something for yourself, too.

Gifts
from the
Garden

The unfortunate truth that all gardeners must accept is that no matter how wonderful a summer garden, the flowers will eventually wither and die. Creative crafters can capture the fresh scents of an abundant garden by using flowers and herbs to make useful and enduring scented gifts.

Hearth Basket

A basket of dried flowers and herbs is a wonderful way to share your summer garden with a fellow crafter. The basket itself, brimming with colorful and fragrant plants, is an attractive decoration—and the bunches of dried materials can be taken out and used as needed.

You Will Need

Large basket

Bunches of dried herbs: bee balm (BB), pink yarrow (Y), silver-king artemisia (SKA), santolina (S), oregano (OR), lamb's-ears (LE), strawflowers (SF), catnip (CAT), lavender (L), and black peppermint (BP)

Rubber bands

Newsprint

Instructions

See page 18 for information on drying herbs and flowers. Bundle dried plants in bunches of 10 to 12 stems and secure stems with rubber bands. Working inward from the basket's rim, layer bunches of fragrant herbs as pictured. Balance colors, textures, and lengths to achieve a pleasing effect.

Design: Alyce Nadeau

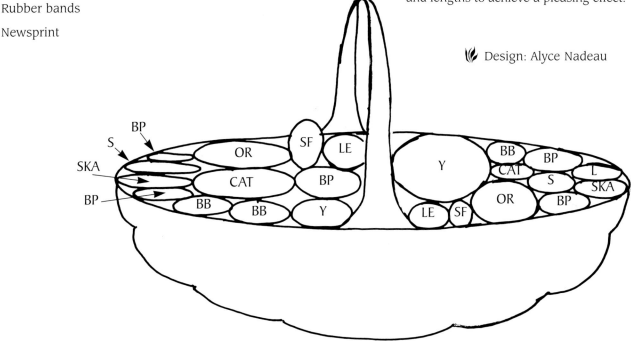

Garden Bounty Herb Wreath

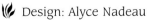

This charming fragrant wreath features the subtle, delicate hues of dried flowers concentrated in the center; an outer rim of artemisia, split-leaf mint, and caspia frames the composition.

You Will Need

25-inch (63.5-cm) birch-twig wreath base

Assorted dried flowers and herbs: artemisia, caspia, split-leaf mint, yarrow, cockscomb, statice, roses, globe amaranth, rudbeckia, baby's breath, strawflowers, and lavender

Floral tape

Floral wire

Hot-glue gun

Instructions

Begin with the outer rim. Break the artemisia into small pieces and form 10 bundles. Wrap the ends of the bundles with floral tape. Apply hot glue to the end of each artemisia bundle and attach to the wreath base. Make sure the artemisia is evenly spaced and that the outer rim of the wreath base is even with the ends of the birch twigs.

Make another 10 bundles out of split-leaf mint and caspia and tape the ends with floral tape. Hot-glue these bundles to the wreath base amongst the artemisia. Next, use floral tape to make bundles of lavender, white yarrow, globe amaranth, and statice. Hot-glue to the wreath base in this order. Continue to hot-glue bundles to wreath until a full look is achieved. Next, use hot glue to randomly place roses, rudbeckia, strawflowers, cockscomb, and baby's breath. Spray finished wreath with a fixative to protect from dust and insects. Attach a wire or ring on the back of the wreath for hanging.

Hint: Lightly misting the dried herbs and flowers with water helps prevent the materials from shattering as you work. Continuing to mist the finished wreath occasionally will keep it fresh as long as possible.

Design: Alyce Nadeau

Gardener's Basket

An assortment of dried aromatics—sweet Annie, lavender, yarrow, miniature roses, and cinnamon sticks—nestled among garden tools is sure to inspire the recipient of this gift basket to get started on a fragrant garden of their own.

You Will Need

Harvest basket

Shredded packing material

Garden gloves

Garden tools (hand rake and hand trowel)

Assorted dried flowers: yellow yarrow, lavender, sweet Annie

Miniature terra-cotta pot

Scented imitation seed packets (available at card shops)

Cinnamon sticks

Artificial butterfly

Raffia

Paper ribbon

For the pomanders

Polystyrene forms in assorted shapes and sizes

Miniature rosebuds

Ribbon

Floral pins

Hot-glue gun

Instructions

First, fill a harvest basket with packing material. You can either wire the items into the basket or simply place them loose in the basket as we've done here. Whether wiring is required will depend on the size and shape of the basket. Gather dried herbs and flowers and separate into small bunches or individual stems. Arrange a bunch of dried lavender in a miniature terra-cotta pot.

To make the rose pomanders, begin by looping a piece of ribbon around a floral pin and inserting the pin into the polystyrene ball to form a hanger. Do this with each of the forms. Beginning at the top of the form (where the hanger is attached), hot-glue miniature roses to the form until the entire surface is covered.

Beginning with the larger items first—the garden tools and gloves, for example—begin to arrange the basket. When all of the larger elements (pomanders, terra-cotta pot, seed packets, and garden tools) are in place, tuck the dried herbs and flowers in between items to fill spaces. Make sure some of the dried material spills out over the edge of the basket.

Tie a group of six or seven cinnamon sticks to the base of the handle with a piece of raffia and hot-glue an artificial butterfly to the edge of the basket, if desired. Tie a bow out of paper ribbon and raffia, and attach to the handle of the basket with raffia. Tuck sprigs of dried lavender into the bow.

🌿 Design: Anne Brightman

Lavender Wands and Bottles

❧

Weaving ribbon through fresh lavender to create bottles (as they were known to the Victorians) is a practice that has been around for centuries. These simple wands are as useful as they are pretty—they can be hung in a closet, tucked in a drawer, or used as a room freshener displayed in a basket or vase. Here are two variations: one to make if you are lucky enough to have fresh lavender, and another, simplified version for dried lavender.

Wrapped Wands

You Will Need

Dried lavender, stalks and flower heads: 20 pieces for each wand

Floral wire

Ribbon in the color of your choice (the length needed will vary)

Instructions

Hold approximately 20 stems of dried lavender in your hand and arrange flower heads so that they form a pleasing bouquet. Once you are happy with the arrangement, wrap floral wire around the stems tightly. Weave ribbon around stems and tie a bow at the base of the stems. Try to obscure the wire with the ribbon, when possible.

Woven Bottles

You Will Need

11, 13, or 15 freshly cut, long-stemmed lavender flowers (must be an odd number)

Ribbon (about 40 inches or 101.5 cm) in the color of your choice (the length needed will vary, depending on the number of lavender stems used)

Instructions

To be certain that the lavender stems will not break whey they are bent, it is best to cut the flowers just before the wand is woven. Do not use dried lavender to make these bottles.

Gather all the flower stems in one hand, holding them near the base of the flower heads. With the other hand, adjust the stems until all the flower heads are level. Tie one end of the ribbon around the stems near the bottom of the flower heads, using a half knot. Leave a 2-inch (5-cm) tail of ribbon on one side of the knot. The remaining long tail will be used for weaving the wand. Adjust all the flower heads by pulling gently on the stems so that the bottom of the flower heads are all resting at the level of the ribbon half knot.

Turn the bundle upside down with the flower heads pointing toward the floor and the stems pointing toward the ceiling. Gently bend each stem over the flower heads, encasing them as if they are to be in a cage of stems. (It's not a major problem if a stem cracks or breaks when it is bent over; the piece, however, will need to be handled carefully for the first two or three rounds of weaving.) Tuck the 2-inch (5-cm) tail of ribbon among the caged flower heads. (Note: the narrower your ribbon width, the more ribbon this project will require.)

Begin weaving the long tail of ribbon over one stem (stem 1) and then under the next stem until stem 13 is reached (or whatever the number of stems that you

are using). You will have made one pass around the cage of stems. To begin the second pass of weaving, place the ribbon under stem 1, then over the next stem, and so forth. This produces the alternate weaving pattern and is why an odd number of stems is necessary. If an even number is used, the alternate pattern will not develop. Also, if you skip a stem on any pass, you will notice it on the next pass when the alternate pattern can't be attained. If this happens, it is best to take out the weaving to the point where the piece was skipped and begin again from that point. Weave tightly, because when the flowers dry, they shrink and the weaving will loosen somewhat.

Once you reach the point where the bundle of flower heads becomes very narrow near the end, stop weaving, wrap the ribbon around all the stems, tie another half knot, then tie a bow with the remaining ribbon. (The bow will have only one tail.) Last, trim the ends of the stems so that they are as even as possible. It is fine to have a few that are a bit short, but the majority should be the same length.

❦ Design: Vicki Baker (wands)
and Sherri Satterwhite (bottles)

Drying Flowers and Herbs

Incorporating dried flowers and herbs into your projects is one of the best ways to create beautiful and long-lasting floral gifts. It's also a great way to make use of a bountiful garden. A wide variety of dried flowers is now available at craft stores and florists, but it is much less expensive (and more satisfying) to dry them yourself. And once you've experimented with drying flowers, you will probably discover that it is addictive.

There are several methods you can use to dry flowers. I prefer using air drying, because it is a more natural process, but you can also use desiccants or a microwave. In principle, all flowers can be dried, though some flowers will keep their shape and hue, and others will fade and shrink considerably. Some flowers retain their scent well after they are dried; others do not. If you want to add scent, it is easy to add a few drops of essential oil to the plant material. Some flower varieties that dry well are blue and red salvia, tansy, cockscomb, strawflowers, lavender, globe amaranth, pansy, statice, hydrangea, larkspur, marigold, zinnia, artemisia, pearly everlasting, and Queen Anne's lace. Consult a flower-drying book for information on drying individual herbs and flowers.

Try to avoid harvesting flowers when they are wet; the point is to get rid of the moisture. Late morning is a good time of day to harvest. Harvest more than you will need, since some of what you pick will be damaged by insects or will get crushed. Store dried flowers away from sunlight, moisture, and insects, preferably in a sealed container.

Air Drying

To air dry using the traditional method, simply secure the stems of freshly cut blooms and hang the bunches upside down in a cool, dark, and nonhumid spot. (One of the advantages of using this method is that the hanging material creates a pleasing decorative effect.) Once the blooms are arranged and hung, you need to check them every couple of days to see if they are completely dried.

Another air drying method is to place the flowers on a wire screen. You will need to turn them periodically to prevent curling. This works well when you want to dry single flowers or leaves or when you are drying flowers with shapes that are not well suited for hanging.

Still another air drying possibility is the upright method, or allowing flowers to dry upright in a vase. This method works well with sturdier flowers, such as statice, and is especially effective for long-stemmed leaves, grasses, and seedpods. Place the container in a warm, dry, dark area. Some flowers, such as hydrangeas, dry better when the vase is filled with water.

Another way to speed up flower drying is to place pans of flowers in a warm 200° F (90° C) oven for several hours. Plant material will retain their shape remarkably, though again, color can change considerably.

Microwave Drying

Using a microwave is, without a doubt, the fastest way to dry flowers. That being said, this drying method takes out most of the scent from the plant material. (If you are planning to add essential oil to the flowers later, this is not a factor.) And because the results are unpredictable, this method can also be frustrating.

Flowers can be dried in a microwave between paper towels, in a paper bag, or with desiccant. (Drying without desiccant is the preferred method of microwave drying.) If you use paper towels, you might need to replace the towels during the drying process; paper bags should be folded closed and placed in a microwave-safe bowl. Consult a flower-drying book for information on how long individual flowers and leaves should be microwaved. Expect to do some experimenting, since microwaves vary widely in their wattage, settings, and performance.

Desiccants

A desiccant is a moisture-absorbing substance. Although sand, borax, yellow cornmeal, and kitty litter are all desiccants, silica gel is the most common desiccant used today to dry flowers.

Place about an inch (2.5 cm) of desiccant in the bottom of a glass or plastic container. Arrange the blooms in the container on top of the silica gel so that they are not touching. You may need to gently pull petals apart to ensure even drying. Check the blooms every three days and remove the flowers as soon as they are dry. Use a small paintbrush to remove any leftover desiccant. You can reuse desiccant, as long as you dry it out between uses.

Pressing

Flower pressing can take anywhere from two to ten weeks. Flower presses are widely available, but you can also use a heavy book or make your own press. Remove the flowers and foliage from the stems and position them on a sheet of blotting (porous) paper; make sure the pieces do not overlap. Place another piece of paper on top of the plants. Carefully place the paper sheets between the pages of a book or in a flower press. See page 58 for gift tags made with pressed flowers.

Finishing

Dried flower arrangements benefit greatly from a coating of clear plastic spray. A dull, clear spray is available in hardware, paint, and craft stores. Hair spray also works well to preserve and protect dried flowers and foliage.

Holiday Lavender Holder

These charming little flower holders are a great holiday project to do with your kids. Display them hung from the fireplace or as delightful place-setting decorations.

You Will Need

Gold doily

Gold tissue paper

Dried lavender

Dried cedar

Holiday ribbon, ¼ inch wide (.5 cm)

Hot-glue gun

Instructions

Paper doilies are available at craft supply stores in a variety of colors and sizes. Fold the doily so that it forms a cone shape and use hot glue to secure one flap over the other. Position gold tissue paper inside the doily. Form a hanger with a length of ribbon by attaching the ribbon ends to each side of the doily holder with dabs of hot glue.

Tie two small bows for the sides and one larger bow for the front of the holder. Hot-glue the bows in place on the sides and front, attaching small pieces of cedar and lavender behind the ribbon, if you like. Fill the holder with loose lavender and place several sprigs of cedar in the back. Fold the tissue down slightly at the front and hot-glue small sprigs of cedar and lavender to the folded-down piece of tissue.

Design: Anne Brightman

Festive Potpourri Box

Using potpourri ingredients to decorate a potpourri container can yield wonderful results. If your potpourri does not lend itself to this technique, you can just as easily use any other dried materials.

You Will Need

Small box

Gold, wire-edged ribbon

Cinnamon sticks

Miniature pine cones

Gold paint (optional)

Dried hydrangea flowers

Holiday potpourri

Hot-glue gun

Instructions

This designer found this charming little box at a craft store, but any small, open-weave container will work just as well—as long as the box allows the scent to escape and the top of the box can be decorated.

First, arrange the gold ribbon on the lid of the box. Create several loops to add interest and allow the ribbon to drape over the sides and corners. Once you are pleased with the design, attach the ribbon with a hot-glue gun. Next, hot-glue the cinnamon sticks to the box. In a few spots, allow the sticks to extend beyond the edge of the box lid and to rest underneath the ribbon.

Cut the hydrangea blooms into small pieces and hot-glue to the box, nestling the flowers among the ribbon and cinnamon sticks. Last, hot-glue an odd number of miniature pine cones in the center of the box top. Fill the box with holiday potpourri.

Design: Mardi Letson

Wedding Potpourri

For the Victorians, the flowers and herbs chosen for potpourri held powerful meaning. A suitor who received a potpourri from his lady would know that marigolds symbolized grief or despair and forget-me-nots true love (see page 36). Each element in this potpourri conveys a wish for a happy and successful married life. We've packaged it in an antique footed bowl, which can be used by the bride and groom for years to come.

You Will Need

Equal portions of the following dried materials: lemon balm leaves, chopped (comfort), red roses (love), pink rosebuds (love), lavender (devotion, luck), rosemary needles (remembrance), baby's breath sprigs (happiness), lunaria membranes (money in your pocket), bay leaves (glory), white yarrow (dreams of loved one), yellow yarrow (dreams of loved one), spearmint leaves (warm feelings), and coxcomb (affection)

Half as much: ivy leaves (love of God) and lemon verbena (unity)

1 yard (.9 m) pink chiffon ribbon

Large, nonmetal container

Decorative glass container

Instructions

In a large, nonmetal container, combine all of the ingredients. Stir gently with your hands until thoroughly mixed. Carefully transfer the potpourri into a decorative container, in this case a footed glass bowl. Tie a bow around the container with a pink chiffon ribbon and cover with plastic wrap before giving.

Design: Alyce Nadeau

Welcome Door Basket

Treat a new neighbor to this lively basket of blooms freshly gathered from your garden.

You Will Need

Wicker door basket

Floral polyfoil

Floral foam

Fresh flowers of your choice

Instructions

Since this is a fresh arrangement and requires moisture, first line the basket with two layers of floral foil to prevent leakage. Next, trim a block of floral foam to fit tightly inside basket, leaving ½ inch (1.5 cm) above the lip of the basket to allow flowers to extend over the edge; this gives the piece an abundant, just-harvested look. Soak the floral foam in water at least an hour, then wedge it into the basket.

We've chosen garden roses, butterfly bush, glossy abelia, artemisia, pennyroyal, chocolate mint, spearmint, and lavender for this basket, but you should use any fragrant flowers and herbs that are blooming in your garden. First, determine the outer perimeter of the arrangement: the height, width, and depth. Establish the shape by inserting the glossy abelia and the mint around the outer edge of the design. Next, determine where you want the focal point of the arrangement to be and insert the larger roses. Fill in the design with the butterfly bush, lavender, and smaller rosebuds and foliage.

🌿 Design: Cathy Lyda Barnhardt

Dried Tussie-Mussie

Tussie-mussies are small posies of fresh or dried flowers that date back to the 1400s, when ladies or gentlemen carried them on their person to perfume their bodies and the air around them. You can choose flowers that express the sentiments you wish to convey (clover for good luck, rosemary for devotion, and so forth—see page 36) or you can simply use the materials you have on hand. If your tussie-mussie does have a special message, include a gift card that lists the plants and their meanings.

You Will Need

Assorted dried flowers (roses, lavender, pennyroyal, tansy, Australian daisies, cockscomb, yarrow, sweet Annie, and dried grasses)

Assorted greenery

Paper doily, 4 inches (10 cm) in diameter

Ribbon, 1 inch wide (2.5 cm), wired

Floral tape

Floral wire

Instructions

Divide the dried flowers and greenery into bunches, then wire each bunch together. Cover the wired stems with floral tape. Choose a prominent flower for the center and surround the center with alternating rings of flower bunches. Bind the stems as you go, keeping the top even to form a mushroom shape. Secure each additional bunch with tape, continuing to add circles until the bouquet reaches approximately 6 inches (15 cm) in diameter.

Frame the posy with a circle of greenery. Make a hole in a paper doily and pull the posy through the hole. Finish by wrapping the stems with a wire-edged ribbon and tying a bow at the base of the doily. Leave several inches of ribbon trailing off the end of the tussie-mussie.

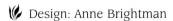 Design: Anne Brightman

Circle of Roses Arrangement

This festive (and long-lasting) arrangement features gorgeous dried scarlet roses
and a painted terra-cotta pot.

You Will Need

Dried roses, red and yellow

4-inch (10-cm) terra-cotta pot

Block of plastic dry foam

Spray paint, burgundy and purple

Spanish moss

Floral pins

Floral tape

Floral wire

Ribbon

Hot-glue gun

Instructions

Spray-paint a 4-inch (10-cm) terra-cotta pot with burgundy paint. When the burgundy paint has dried, spray-paint the pot again with a light coat of purple paint. Allow to dry thoroughly. Cut a piece of plastic foam to fit inside pot and glue into place. Cover foam with Spanish moss and secure moss with floral pins.

Place wire against the stems of the roses and wrap stems and wire with floral tape. Insert the larger red roses into the foam. Fill in with smaller roses—in this case, smaller red roses and miniature yellow roses. Vary the placement of the flowers so as to create an interesting arrangement. Wrap the pot with ribbon and tie a bow. Hot-glue ribbon to pot in spots to secure.

 Design: Anne Brightman

Flower-Adorned Garden Hat

What could be simpler than a gardener's hat that displays the yield from last-year's flower garden? Although it will certainly shield the weary plower from the sun, this hat is also gorgeous on a door or wall.

You Will Need

Straw hat

Assorted dried flowers (sweet Annie, plumosa fern, globe amaranth, and caspia)

Floral tape

Plastic-coated electrical wire, 14-gauge

Needle-nose pliers

Instructions

The amount of materials you will need will depend on the size and shape of the hat you choose. First, make miniature bouquets from the dried materials. Separate pieces of each type of flower and gather together in a bunch with the stems together. Wrap floral tape around the stems. Depending on the hat, you will probably need 15 to 20 bouquets.

Next, measure the rim of the hat; add ½ inch (1.5 cm) to the measurement and cut a piece of electrical wire to that length. Wrap floral tape snugly around the wire to form a base for the bouquets. Starting at one end of the wire, place each bouquet, one after the other, against the wrapped wire and secure to the wire with floral tape. You will need to tightly draw the tape to ensure a snug hold.

Once the entire piece of wire is covered with flowers, use needle-nose pliers to form a loop at each end of the wire. Wrap the garland of flowers around the rim of the hat and connect the loops. If the loops are visible, hot-glue a bow at the point where the loops join.

🌿 Design: Vicki Baker

Miniature Herb Garden

A small herb garden makes a useful gift for a friend who enjoys herbal cooking and crafting. This is also an inexpensive present, since many herbs can be rooted or divided from your own mature plants.

You Will Need

9-inch-deep (23-cm) terra-cotta pot

Assorted small herb plants and cuttings

Potting soil

Craft sticks

Instructions

Use any well-drained potting soil. If any of the plants are tender, choose plants that grow well inside, since the garden will have to be brought in for the winter. (Basil is the example here.) Whatever herbs you choose, you will need to provide instructions for how to grow each. We've included basil, rosemary, clary sage, nutmeg-scented geranium, and thyme.

Basil can be grown from seed (it takes four to five weeks), cuttings can be taken from more mature basil plants, or small plants can be purchased. To root from new growth, cut off all but the top four leaves, stick the cutting in moist soil, and keep moist. Don't give the plant intense light until it has rooted. Root rosemary in moist soil from cuttings of new growth or buy small plants. Take cuttings of sage in the fall and root in moist soil or divide new growth for small sage plants.

Scented geraniums can be rooted in water. Thyme can be grown from seed, divided from mature plants, or rooted in wet soil.

Write the names of the plants on craft sticks and stick in soil near plants; be careful not to damage the roots by inserting the stick too close to the plant. Let the recipient know that the plants will grow well in this pot for a while, but if they're going to be kept potted indefinitely, some of the plants will need to be separated out to give room for the others. (The basil will last only a year, which will provide some space.)

Design: Patrick Doran

Planning a Fragrant Garden

The first whiff of blooming flowers in early spring is one of life's simple pleasures. And a garden filled with deliciously scented plants makes putting together a fragrant gift much easier. Here are some tips for creating an aromatic garden.

First, it's important when planning a fragrant garden not to try to pack too many conflicting scents into a small space. Try to stick to families of scents: fruity, woody, or spicy, for example. Choose your plants carefully so that only two or three plants are releasing a scent in any season.

Yellow Yarrow

Bee Balm

Windowboxes make superb miniature scented gardens—if you plan them carefully, the scent will greet you inside the house. Arbors, trellises, and overhangs can become wonderful scented areas when draped with a climbing scented plant, such as honeysuckle, roses, and wisteria.

Don't forget to include plants that have scented foliage. Mint comes in a glorious variety of scents—although most do not release their scent until their leaves are touched (see page 70). Try grouping plants with similarly scented leaves together: lemon thyme, lemon-scented geraniums, lemon grass, lemon verbena, and lemon balm, for example. Another idea is to plan a garden intended solely for making potpourri, including, for example, pineapple mint, scented geraniums, roses, and lavender. Or place rose-scented flowers and foliage in or near your rose garden to increase the effect.

Anise Hyssop

Overall, a scented garden needs a fair amount of sun exposure. (Warmth releases the scent and most scented plants are sun-lovers.) In addition, the air in your fragrant garden must be reasonably still, since strong winds will disperse the scent; so provide shelter for your plants. Consider planting evergreen and deciduous trees and shrubs—they must be somewhat porous, so as not to create a wind tunnel—to serve as windbreaks.

Placing your fragrance garden near a bench or other outdoor seating helps to make enjoying your scented garden convenient and relaxing. Try to put your scented flowers as close to nose height as possible, even if you have to raise them above the ground. Scented leaves and foliage should be positioned so that hands and feet can access them easily, since these scents are often released when they are brushed against or touched. Pathways and borders are great spots for scented plants.

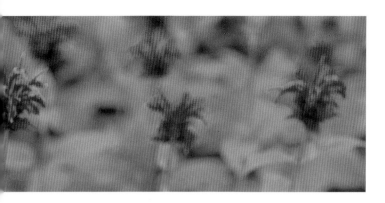

If you do not have the time or the patience to plant a fragrant garden, you can force fragrant blooms indoors. Daffodils, freesia, hyacinths, Easter liles, and narcissuses are a few of the scented bulbs you can force. And containers brimming with spring bulbs make wonderful winter gifts.

Here's a list of just a few of the scented plants you might consider planting in your garden: sweet pea, sweet alyssum, sweet sultan, stock, clary sage, dame's rocket, sweet William, wallflower, lavender, chamomile, yarrow, garden phlox, lily of the valley, peony, pinks, orris root, sweet violet, snow white bee balm, nasturtiums, scented geraniums, azaleas, monarda, anise hyssop, butterfly bush, salvia, costmary, catnip, and roses.

When planted nearby, yarrow is said to increase fragrance in other plants.

Pink Yarrow

Chamomile

Pomanders

Pomanders, or spheres adorned with spices or flowers, have been around since medieval times, when they were worn or carried to ward off disease. They have also been used in closets, wardrobes, and dresser drawers for their aromatic properties and as a moth deterrent. See page 15 for rosebud pomanders.

Lavender Pomander

You Will Need

3-inch (7.5-cm) polystyrene ball

Lavender flowers

Pink larkspur flowers

Floral pin

⅓ yard (.3 m) ½-inch-wide (1.5-cm) satin ribbon

Paintbrush

White craft glue

Hot-glue gun

Instructions

Pour lavender flowers onto a flat, clean surface. With a paintbrush, paint the surface of the foam ball with white craft glue and gently roll ball in lavender flowers until the ball is completely coated. Allow to dry thoroughly. Use a floral pin to attach a loop of ribbon to the ball as a hanger. Beginning with the top (where the ribbon in attached), use hot-glue gun to place pink larkspur in a strip around the entire length of the ball. Hot-glue additional larkspur randomly among the lavender flowers. For a variation, mix other flower petals with lavender before rolling the ball in glue.

Bay Leaf Kitchen Pomander

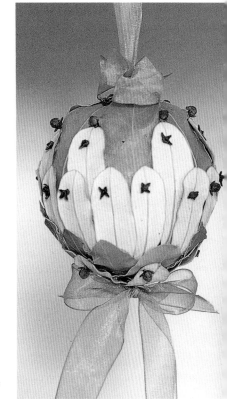

You Will Need

3-inch (7.5-cm) polystyrene ball

Bay leaves, approximately 15 leaves

Mesquite leaves, approximately 18 leaves

Cloves, approximately 30

1 yard (.9 m) 1-inch-wide (2.5-cm) organza ribbon

Floral pins

Hot-glue gun

Instructions

Hot-glue a layer of bay leaves to the foam ball so that an entire half of the ball is covered with leaves. Using a floral pin, attach a loop of organza ribbon at the top of the ball (where it is covered with bay leaves) to serve as a hanger. Arrange mesquite leaves on the bottom half of the ball in a pleasing pattern and hot-glue in place. Hot-glue small bay leaves at the very bottom of the ball, with the bay leaves covering the bottom edges of the mesquite leaves. Tie a bow with the remainder of the ribbon and attach bow to the bottom of the ball with another floral pin. Make small holes in the ball with a toothpick or heavy-gauge wire, then insert cloves.

Purple Pomander

You Will Need

3-inch (7.5-cm) poly-styrene ball

Lavender flowers

Purple lark-spur flowers

3 yellow sweetheart roses

Floral pin

⅓ yard (.3 m) ½-inch-wide (1.5-cm) gold ribbon

Instructions

Pour lavender flowers onto a flat, clean surface. With a paintbrush, paint the surface of the foam ball with white craft glue and gently roll ball in lavender flowers until the ball is completely coated. Allow to dry thoroughly. Use a floral pin to attach a loop of ribbon to the ball. Beginning with the top (where the ribbon in attached), use hot-glue gun to place purple larkspur flowers in four strips down the sides of the ball. Hot-glue sprigs of lavender, tansy, yellow sweetheart roses, and purple larkspur at the base of the hanger.

A simple and quite fragrant variation is to stud citrus fruits (here, we've used oranges) with cloves. Push whole cloves into the fruit, leaving space between the cloves. (You may want to use a darning needle or ice pick to puncture the fruit's skin.) Dust citrus pomanders with powdered spices for additional scent. Allow to dry for four weeks.

Sweetheart Pomander

You Will Need

2-inch (5-cm) polystyrene ball

Pink larkspur flowers

Sweet Annie

Sweetheart rosebuds

Floral pin

⅓ yard (.3 m) ¼-inch-wide (.5-cm) satin ribbon

Hot-glue gun

Instructions

Hot-glue sweetheart rosebuds to the foam ball in no particular order. Fill in spaces between roses with pink larkspur, again using a hot-glue gun to attach the blooms. Attach a loop of ribbon to the top of the ball with a floral pin, then hot-glue sprigs of sweet Annie around the base of the hanger.

Note: You can enhance the fragrance of any of these pomanders with a few drops of essential oil.

❦ Design: Cathy Lyda Barnhardt

Seashell Arrangement

A treasure brought home from the beach houses a dried flower arrangement and offers a fond (and fragrant) reminder of the trip. In composing the arrangement, the designer tried to echo the rhythms and colors of the ocean.

You Will Need

Large seashell

Plastic container

Floral foam

Sheet moss

Floral pins

Assorted dried flowers (tansy, blue delphinium, lavender, and sweet Annie)

Instructions

A plastic container helps to contain the dry floral foam (which tends to be brittle); here, we've used a butter container, but any container that fits inside the shell will work just as well. Cut a piece of floral foam to fit the container, then wedge the container into the shell. Cover all exposed surfaces of the container and foam with sheet moss and secure moss with floral pins.

Break dried materials into individual stems and clusters and begin to insert into floral foam. Start with the longer, spiked stems in the back of the design—the lavender and the sweet Annie—then fill in the front with tansy and blue delphinium. If the stems are difficult to work with, attach them to floral picks.

🌿 Design: Cathy Lyda Barnhardt

Rose Beads

Beads made from the petals of fragrant roses release a fabulous scent when worn against the skin. And surprisingly enough, rose beads last a long time; this designer has had one set for 15 years.

You Will Need

5 cups (70 g) rose petals

Rose essential oil

1 gallon (3.8 l) distilled spring water

Blender or food processor

Glass bowl

Straight pins

Cork board

Needle

Bead-stringing thread

Instructions

Collect rose petals in the early morning on a dry day. Discard any brown or wilted petals. Cut petals into small pieces and place in a saucepan with just enough water to cover the rose pieces. Cook over low heat and simmer until water has cooked away. Cover with water again and cook down again over low heat.

Process the cooked rose pieces in a blender or a food processor until mixture becomes a paste. Add some water, if necessary. Getting the right consistency is sometimes difficult, but don't give up. Transfer the paste to a glass bowl.

Put rose oil on your fingers. Separate a small portion of the paste and roll in the palm of your hand until a bead is formed. While the paste is still wet, stick a straight pin through the bead to form a hole and stick pin (with bead still on it) on cork board. Allow to dry for approximately one week. Rotate the beads on the pins occasionally to prevent sticking.

When the beads are thoroughly dry, remove the straight pin and spread the beads out on a flat surface. Allow the inner surfaces of the pinholes to dry for another day or two. Thread a needle with nylon bead-stringing thread and double the thread. Insert the needle through the holes in the beads and string the beads together. Attach finding to the ends or tie in a simple knot. Combine rose beads with other beads, if you like. Store in a glass jar with a cotton ball that has been soaked in rose oil to maintain the scent.

Design: Corky Kurzmann

Common Fragrant Plants and Spices

Anise hyssop *(Hyssopus officinalis)*

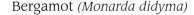

Scent: Spicy, warm, nicely aromatic

Symbolizes: Cleanliness

Effect: Relaxes, soothes, aids respiratory system

Ancients held this plant sacred through the ages. It has been prescribed for its healing effects on the respiratory system; ancient pharmacopeia included it as a major ingredient in many preparations, elixirs, and syrups.

Basil, sweet *(Ocimum basilicum)*

Scent: Pleasant, anisey, with a trace of mint

Symbolizes: Best wishes, warm friendship

Effect: Uplifts, awakens, clarifies, stimulates

Considered an aphrodisiac by the Romans and incorporated into many culinary recipes. Holds a more sacred status in India, where the herb is dedicated to the god Vishnu and is used extensively in Ayurvedic medicine.

Bay, sweet *(Laurus nobilis)*

Scent: Strong, masculine, clovelike, woody

Symbolizes: Memory, reward of merit, loyalty

Effect: Antiseptic, toning, mild sedative

Bay oil was highly valued for its use as a remedy for hair loss and is an essential ingredient in the bay rum used by men in the Victorian age to wash and dress their hair.

Bergamot *(Monarda didyma)*

Scent: Sweet, citrusy, with a hint of floral

Symbolizes: Confidence, balance, strength, harmony

Effect: Brings joy, refreshes, encourages, relaxes

Though the essence of this fragrance comes from the rind of a bitter orange tree, its name may actually have come from bergamot pears, a species so-called for the Turkish *beg-armudi*, meaning "bey's pear."

Carnation *(Dianthus caryophyllus)*

Scent: Clovelike, some varieties are unscented

Symbolizes: Refusal, disdain, secretiveness, independence, stillness, tenderness

Effect: Liberates and comforts

The name of this flower first appeared in 1538 as "Incarnacyon." Others called it coronation, either due to its toothed petals, which resemble crowns, or to the former Greek tradition of weaving its blossoms into garlands.

Chamomile *(Chamaemelum nobile)*

Scent: Fresh, applelike

Symbolizes: Meekness, resignation

Effect: Relaxes, soothes, encourages patience, peaceful, calming

The fascinating history of this scented treasure includes a now-famous tomb; chamomile was found to be the main herb constituent in the embalming oil used to mummify Ramses II in 1224 BC.

Cinnamon
(Cinnamomum zeylanicum)

Scent: Spicy, warm

Symbolizes: Benevolence, steadfastness, energy

Effect: Warms

Hardly a prescription seems to have been issued without mention of this spice by the ancients in China, where cinnamon was revered as a tranquilizer, tonic, and a good spice for a weak heart. Arab traders supplied this invaluable spice to the Greeks and Romans, but the secret of its origins became so highly coveted that it spurred the Portuguese to seek out a route around the Cape to India and Ceylon in the sixteenth century.

Clary Sage *(Salvia sclarea)*

Scent: Warm, nutty

Symbolizes: Esteem, friendship

Effect: Euphoric, restorative; eases menstrual pain and PMS

Deriving from the Latin *salvere*, meaning "to save," this herb was valued by the Romans, Greeks, and Egyptians for its healing properties. The Latin *clarus*, or "clear," led to the name "clary," meaning clear eye, which was derived from the herb's early use as a treatment for blurry vision.

Clove *(Syzygium aromaticum)*

Scent: Hot, spicy

Symbolizes: Dignity

Effect: Good for toothaches and sore throats; strengthens memory, antiseptic

While Europeans used cloves in pomanders to ward off the plague during the Renaissance, courtiers of the Han court in second-century China sucked on cloves to sweeten their breath when appearing before the emperor.

Coriander *(Coriandrum sativum)*

Scent: Musky, aromatic

Symbolizes: Concealed merit

Effect: Enlivens, motivates, encourages

Considered one of the oldest flavorings in the world, coriander at one time played a large role in obstetrics: it was once believed that a woman could stop menstruating and quickly become pregnant by taking the seeds regularly, and that a few seeds placed at the top of a woman's thigh during labor would facilitate birth and ease pain.

Eucalyptus *(Eucalyptus)*

Scent: Fresh, balsamic, camphoric

Symbolizes: Emotional balance, centering, logical thought, predictability

Effect: Stimulates, balances, shelters

Eucalyptus has been regarded as a powerful cure-all for centuries. A native of Australia, the herb's medicinal uses date back as far as that country's indigenous Aborigine cultures, and were later discovered by white settlers.

Fennel *(Foeniculum vulgare)*

Scent: Strong, anisey, camphoric, similar to licorice

Symbolizes: Worthy of all praise, fortitude, perseverance, forcefulness, courage, reliability

Effect: Clears, enlightens, motivates

Valued since ancient times as a condiment and medicine, fennel has also long been appreciated for its ability to stimulate the flow of breast milk. On a different note, people in the Middle Ages used fennel to prevent witchcraft and ward off evil spirits.

Frankincense *(Boswellia sacra)*

Scent: Spicy, woody, slightly lemony

Symbolizes: Introspection, comfort, inspiration, emotional stability

Effect: Elevating, meditative, spiritual, calming

In the Bible, one of the spices presented by the wise men to baby Jesus. Burned in the ancient temples of Babylon, Egypt, Greece, and Rome, frankincense was deemed "worth its weight in gold," literally. It's extracted from the tree *Boswellia sacra*.

Geranium, Scented *(Pelargonium)*

Scent: Strong, sweet, roselike

Symbolizes: Comfort, humor, security, mothering, shielding

Effect: Balances, heals, uplifts, comforts

The name of this plant bears a fascinating lineage, originating from the title "Odin's Grace," which celebrated the supreme deity of Norse mythology. Next came the German "Gottesdagne," which gave way to the Old English "Gratia Dei," or "gift of God," as John Gerard referred to the plant in the sixteenth century. Colonial women often plucked bunches of marigolds and scented geraniums to take to church—the pungent aroma of the bouquets gave them a wide-awake look during long sermons! See also page 74.

Ginger *(Zingiber officinale)*

Scent: Camphorlike, aromatic, citrusy

Symbolizes: Confidence, warmth, fortitude, empathy, courage

Effect: Warms, strengthens, encourages

Ginger's healing effects have been utilized by doctors of all times and places: medieval physicians used the spice to combat the Black Death—it provoked sweating—and witch doctors on the Pacific Island of Dohu continue to chew the root and spit it into patients' wounds and burns to heal their ailments. Said to soothe urinary infections.

Jasmine *(Jasminum)*

Scent: Deep, sweet, warming, exhilarating, exotic

Symbolizes: Joy, grace, sensuality

Effect: Aphrodisiac, uplifts, aids sleep, balances, an antidepressant

One of the most sensual scents nature has to offer, jasmine was revered as the oil of romance in the Hindu and Muslim traditions. The favorite of the prince's harem bathed in a jasmine-perfumed bath and received a jasmine massage, both of which were supposed to induce sensual ecstasy in her lover.

Lavender *(Lavendula)*

Scent: Clean, classic, appeasing

Symbolizes: Distrust, silence

Effect: Relaxes, calms, heals

Roman bathers used the fragrant oil of lavender to perfume their baths, thus giving it its name: the Latin word *lavandus* means "to be washed." The infusion of the scent in modern soaps dates to 1671, when William Yardley of Surrey took over the soap holdings of James I and began adding lavender to the recipe, making for a much sweeter smelling populace. See also page 49.

Lemon *(Lemonia)*

Scent: Citrusy

Symbolizes: Joy, liveliness, clarity, direction, awareness

Effect: Purifies, stimulates

Although the ancients used the peel of the lemon to perfume their clothes and act as a pesticide, this jewel of the citrus family gained most of its glory when it was issued to the British Navy to combat the effects of scurvy, earning inhabitants of Britain the erroneous nickname "limey."

Lovage *(Levisticum officinale)*

Scent: Musky, earthy

Symbolizes: Unknown

Effect: Cleanses, aids digestion

Popular in the Middle Ages, when it was used for culinary and medicinal purposes. Though the Emperor Charlemagne included the herb in his garden, lovage has fallen from favor among modern gardeners. With a thick, hollow stem and large leaves that look and taste like celery, it's no wonder lovage is also known as bastard celery in France. The English are slightly more kind, referring to the herb as love parsley.

Marjoram, sweet *(Origanum majorana)*

Scent: Warm, spicy, sweet, appeasing

Symbolizes: Happiness, joy

Effect: Calms, sedates, an antiseptic

Greeks and Romans wove crowns of marjoram to adorn the newly married, while Aphrodite, goddess of love and fecundity in Greek mythology, picked marjoram on Mount Ida to heal the wounds of her son Aeneas. (It apparently had no scent until she touched it.)

Mint *(Mentha)*

Scent: Sweet, minty, refreshing

Symbolizes: Virtue, wisdom

Effect: Refreshes emotions, stimulates, penetrates, awakens

See page 70.

Myrrh *(Commiphora molmol)*

Scent: Strong, balsamic, musty, hint of camphor

Symbolizes: Gladness

Effect: Stimulates, fortifies, good for skin problems (revitalizes, tones) and for throat and gum problems

The Egyptian papyri, the Vedas, the Bible, and the Koran all mention the oil of this spiky shrub as an ingredient in many elixirs, incenses, and multipurpose antidotes. The Hebrews mixed myrrh in their wine to raise their state of consciousness before religious ceremonies, and administered the same concoction to criminals to ease their mental anguish before execution.

Myrtle *(Myrtus communis)*

Scent: Fresh-smelling, similar to eucalyptus

Symbolizes: Love, a first declaration of love

Effect: Stimulates, uplifts, good for skin care

A powerful astringent, the cleansing properties of myrtle's leaves and flowers were widely celebrated in the sixteenth century, when they served in the preparation of a renowned tonic called "angel water."

Neroli *(Citrus sinensis)*

Scent: Sweet, citrusy

Symbolizes: Bridal festivities; chastity

Effect: Warming and sensual; relaxing and also stimulating

Oil extracted from the Seville orange tree. Before orange perfumes came to symbolize purity, neroli reigned as the favored scent of Madrid's prostitutes—customers could recognize them by their scent.

Nutmeg *(Myristica fragrans)*

Scent: Spicy, peppery

Symbolizes: Unknown

Effect: Powerful stimulant and tonic; aphrodisiac

After being brought to the Mediterranean by Arab traders in the twelfth century, nutmeg remained the monopoly of the Portuguese and then the Dutch for many years. The reign of the "Spice Islands" was broken in 1768, when several young trees were smuggled out by Pierre Poivre, which led to a thriving nutmeg crop in the West Indies.

Patchouli *(Pogostemon cablin)*

Scent: Strong, sweet, musty, very persistent

Symbolizes: Persistence, lucidity, restoration, invigoration

Effect: Soothes, reassures, grounds; in the East, a renowned antidote against insect and snake bites.

Indians often used patchouli to scent their fabrics, as the English learned in the nineteenth century, when the famous Indian shawls became fashionable.

Pine *(Pinus)*

Scent: Strong, camphoric, balsamic

Symbolizes: Pity

Effect: Encourages patience, acceptance, and understanding

With trunks towering over 120 feet (36 m) in height, pine trees have historically been a prime candidate for sailing ship masts. Its kernels and nuts have also proved useful—excavated Roman dwellings in Britain show traces of pine kernel and nut husks, suggesting the plant's value as both food and medicine.

Rose *(Rosa)*

Scent: Sweet and rosy

Symbolizes: True love, devotion, patience, sensuality, silence

Effect: Relaxes; sometimes considered an aphrodisiac

Treasured by the Romans and Greeks, roses have been valued throughout history worldwide for their sweet smell, lovely hues, and gorgeous blooms.

Rosemary *(Rosmarinus officinalis)*

Scent: Fiery, aromatic, invigorating

Symbolizes: Remembrance, devotion

Effect: Restores, centers, strengthens

This herb had the honor to appear in many prized formulas during the Middle Ages and Renaissance, one being the famous "water of the queen of Hungary." After Elizabeth of Hungary received the recipe for this rejuvenating liquor from an angel or a monk at age seventy-two, her gout and paralysis were displaced by her former health and beauty to such an extent that the king of Poland reportedly wished to marry her!

Sandalwood *(Santalum album)*

Scent: Sweet, fruity, woody

Symbolizes: Warmth, comfort, sensitivity, serenity, insight

Effect: Aids meditation, balances, connects, reduces nervous tension

Sandlewood is native to the province of Mysore in India. There is record of sandalwood in Chinese and Sanskrit manuscripts. Ancient Egyptians used the wood in embalming, medicine, and ritual and even carved objects from it. The tree has to be thirty years old before its essentail oil is fully developed

Thyme *(Thymus)*

Scent: Hot, spicy, aromatic

Symbolizes: Activity

Effect: Invigorates, empowers

The name comes from the Greek word *thumos* (to smell). Thyme is known for its insect-repellant properties, and Romans even burned this herb outside their houses to keep reptiles away. Since they also believed in its ability to dispel melancholy and promote bravery, Roman soldiers bathed in thyme before going to battle.

Vetiver *(Vetiveria zizanioides)*

Scent: Warm, peppery, spicy, woody, earthy

Symbolizes: Integrity, wisdom, mind-body connection, self-esteem

Effect: Grounds, centers

Known as *khus-khus* or *khas-khas* in India, this aromatic oil comes from vetiver grass, a species cultivated in tropical and subtropical climates. The strong scent of the plant lies not in its narrow leaves, but in its roots, which possess a fragrance similar to violets or sandalwood.

Ylang-Ylang *(Cananga odorata)*

Scent: Sweet, exotic

Symbolizes: Self-confidence, warmth, enthusiasm, unification

Effect: Euphoric, sensual; stimulates, soothes, and relaxes; creates balance

Appropriately named "flower of flowers," the ylang-ylang tree yields a host of beautiful, highly fragrant yellow flowers responsible for many a sweet sigh in Indonesia, where people adorn the beds of newly-weds with the blossoms on their wedding night.

Yarrow *(Achillea Millefolium)*

Scent: Strong, earthy

Symbolizes: War

Effect: Analgesic, anti-inflammatory

Though yarrow has been prescribed to treat almost every ailment known to man, it has traditionally been very popular among American Indians. They used the plant for everything from an eyewash to a laxative.

Gifts
that
Pamper

Don't resist gift-giving just because there's no special occasion. The most treasured gifts are often unexpected. This section is full of gift ideas for the friend who would love nothing better than to relax in a hot, bubbly, and aromatic bath.

Spanish Bubble Bath

❦

This gentle bubble-bath formula is made with castile soap, which originated in Castile, Spain, and can be found in most health food stores. The recipe also includes olive oil, long valued for its wonderful skin-moisturizing qualities.

You Will Need

1 tablespoon (15 ml) castile soap

½ cup (119 ml) boiling water

½ teaspoon olive oil

A few drops of an essential oil: patchouli, eucalyptus, sandalwood, or any oil of your choice (optional)

Mixing bowl

Whisk

Antique glass bottle or other container

Instructions

Although this bubble bath is not exceptionally bubbly, it leaves skin smooth and silky. With a whisk, beat all of the ingredients together in a mixing bowl until the mixture is frothy. Pour into a container—a pretty glass bottle or any other attractive container of your choice. Attach a tag to the bottle instructing the recipient to add 2 to 3 tablespoons of bubble bath to the bath, shaking well prior to each use. The shelf life of this bubble bath is about one month.

🌿 Design: Casey Kellar

For additional recipes and information on natural cosmetics, see Kellar's book, The Natural Bath & Beauty Book *(Lark, 1997).*

Relaxing English Bath Salts

Epsom salts, which get their name from the mineral springs in Epsom, England (where they were first discovered), are known for their ability to relieve sore and tired muscles. Combine them with lavender, which relaxes and soothes, and you have easy-to-make bath salts—the perfect gift for an overworked friend.

You Will Need

¾ cup (240 g) Epsom salts

¼ cup (80 g) sea salt

¼ cup (7 g) dried lavender

Cheesecloth or other loose-weave fabric (optional)

String or twine (optional)

Decorative bottle (optional)

Instructions

The sea salt helps soak off dead skin cells and tones the skin, while lavender provides relaxing aromatherapy value to the bath. (You should be able to find sea salt at your local health food store; if not, try stores carrying aquarium supplies.) To make the salts, mix all the ingredients together.

If you wish, spoon two to three spoonfuls of the mixture into a piece of cheesecloth or any other loose-weave fabric. Gather the top of the fabric and tie with a piece of string or twine to create a bath sachet. This quantity makes seven to ten sachets. (The fabric container keeps the lavender from floating all over the bath and makes cleanup easy.)

Or you can put the salts in a decorative bottle or other container as we've done here and provide the recipient with instructions for making the sachets. The sachet should be tossed into running bath water and allowed to steep for three to five minutes. The shelf life is about one year.

 Design: Casey Kellar

For additional recipes and information on natural cosmetics, see Kellar's book, The Natural Bath & Beauty Book *(Lark, 1997).*

Garden Oils

This body oil makes a fantastic gift, especially if bottled in a clear container. You can substitute dried herbs, such as rosemary, chamomile, mint, wintergreen, or sage, for dried flowers in this recipe, but be aware that herbs sometimes provide additional fragrance to the blend.

You Will Need

¼ cup (60 ml) safflower oil

¼ cup (60 ml) sweet almond oil

2 drops vitamin E

¼ cup (4 g) dried rose petals

1 sprig of pink, purple, or white dried larkspur

A few drops of rose essential oil (optional)

Raffia

Instructions

All flowers must be completely dried (not fresh) and free of any insects, debris, or additives. If you don't want to dry your own flowers, you can buy them from specialty growers, order them from a local florist, or find them at harvest festivals. Do not use flowers from commercial potpourri.

Arrange a few of the flowers and petals in the bottle. Do not put too many flowers in the bottle, as it will overcrowd the container and ruin the effect. Next, blend the oils together (safflower, almond, and vitamin E). Fill your bottle with the blended oils, and add the essential oil last. (Single petals are likely to float until they become saturated.) Tie a raffia bow around bottle.

The flowers themselves will not impart any fragrance to your oil, because they are dried; however, the oil will preserve the flowers, which add decorative effect to the bottle. The oil should be shaken a few times before using and has a shelf life of about one year.

Design: Casey Kellar

For additional recipes and information on natural cosmetics, see Kellar's book, The Natural Bath & Beauty Book *(Lark, 1997).*

Herbal Bath Vinegars

These vinegars make for a relaxing and fragrant bath and can be created using any fresh herb from your garden, such as chamomile, lavender, rosemary, thyme, and mint.

You Will Need

2 cups (200 g) dried herbs

1 quart (.9 l) of white wine vinegar

Microwave-safe bowl

Decorative bottles

Ribbon, raffia, and dried herbs
for decorating bottles

Instructions

Place 2 cups (200 g) of dried herbs in a microwave-safe bowl. Pour 1 quart (.9 l) of white wine vinegar over the herbs and bring to a boil in the microwave oven on high power. (Although it is much easier to use a microwave, you can bring the mixture to a boil on the stove top as well.) Remove from the microwave and allow to cool.

Pour mixture of vinegar and herbs into jar and cover. Allow the vinegar mixture to steep for two weeks, shaking daily. Strain off herbs and place into pretty bottles. Decorate with ribbon, raffia, and dried herbs as desired. Attach a tag with this recipe and instructions to add several drops of herbal vinegar to hot bath water.

❦ Design: Anne Brightman

Oatmeal Cinnamon Soap

Although making soap from scratch is time consuming, it is not difficult. And soapmakers all agree that it is an extremely satisfying process. A kitchen scale is indispensable, because all of the basic ingredients must be measured by weight—even the liquids.

You Will Need

3 pounds (1.4 kg) cold distilled water or spring water

1 pound (454 g) of 100% lye

2 pounds, 12 ounces (1.2 kg) coconut oil

1 pound, 12 ounces (794 g) palm or hardened vegetable oil

3 pounds, 8 ounces (1.6 kg) olive oil

4 ounces (113 g) wheat germ oil

2,000 IU vitamin E, in capsule form

1½ cups (700 g) oatmeal

2 tablespoons cinnamon leaf oil

3 teaspoons ground cinnamon

2 glass jars

Kitchen scale

Cardboard box

Wax paper

Rubber spatula

8-quart (7.6-l) enamel pot

3-quart (2.8-l) enamel pot

Candy or meat thermometer

Small mixing bowl

Muslin and raffia for packaging

Instructions

To prepare the mold, line a cardboard box with wax paper so that the entire bottom and 3 inches (7.5 cm) of the sides are covered two layers thick. For these bars, the designer used a box that is 25½ x 13½ x 5 inches (64.5 x 34 x 12.5 cm), which yields forty-two 4-ounce (113-g) bars of soap.

Note: It is best to have equipment that is reserved for use only with soapmaking. If this is not possible, make sure the pots and utensils are thoroughly cleaned after each batch of soap. You should use only nonmetal equipment when mixing soap, as metal will react with the lye. After the soap has hardened, however, it is fine to use a metal knife or ruler to cut the bars.

Put on rubber gloves and goggles. Measure 3 pounds (1.4 l) of water in a ½-gallon (1.9 l) glass jar, then measure 1 pound (455 g) of lye in a separate glass jar. Pour lye slowly and carefully into water, then stir with rubber spatula until clear. This mixture gets very hot (200° F or 93° C) and is the most dangerous part of soapmaking. Make sure you *pour the lye into the water*, not the other way around. Clean up the area immediately. Cover lye mixture with lid and set aside to cool for about an hour and a half.

Measure coconut oil and palm/vegetable oil into an 8-quart (7.6-l) enamel pot and put over slow heat to melt. (Coconut oil and palm oil are both solids.) In a separate 3-quart (2.8-l) enamel pot, measure olive oil, wheat germ oil, and vitamin E; these are liquid and do not require melting. Once the palm oil mixture is melted, take off the heat. Pour the cool olive oil mixture into the hot palm oil mixture. You will need to use a candy or a meat thermometer to measure the temperature of both the oil mixture and the lye mixture.

When both mixtures are between 80° to 100° F (27° to 38° C), slowly pour the lye mixture into the oil mixture while stirring constantly in a linear motion. (Do not whip, stir in circles, or scrape sides.) Continue stirring until the mixture thickens enough to leave a faint raised trail on the surface when you lift the spatula out of the liquid. This should take about 10 minutes.

Combine the oatmeal and cinnamon in a separate bowl, then slowly mix into soap until completely blended. Pour in cinnamon leaf essential oil and stir until blended. The entire mixture should be uniform in color—not streaky. Pour entire contents of pot into lined mold (already-prepared cardboard box) without scraping sides of pot. Cover the mold with additional cardboard and place blankets on top to keep warm. Set aside for three to five days.

Uncover and expose to air for an additional five days. After five days, scrape off top white layer of soap by pulling the side of a metal ruler along the entire length of the box. This should take off about a ⅛-inch (.3-cm) layer of soda ash or lye residue. The soap should be brown underneath.

Measure soap into bars of the desired size by marking lines with a ruler and a knife. Cut carefully along the marks, using a very sharp knife and a ruler as a guide. Gently flip the entire box over to release bars from the cardboard mold. Place individual bars of soap, right side up, on cardboard that is covered with the unprinted sides of paper bags. Make sure the bars are not touching each other. Allow the soap to sit for at least three weeks.

Once the soap is dry, wrap each bar with muslin and tie with raffia.

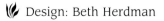 Design: Beth Herdman

LAVENDER

The gorgeous hues, pleasing shape, and unmistakable aroma of lavender make it an ideal ingredient for a variety of scented gifts. Although lavender has traditionally been used in sachets (often to scent linen and protect it from moths), it has been known for its healing and antiseptic qualities since Roman times. It has been used to treat lice, hysteria, nervous palpitations, hoarseness, palsy, toothaches, sore joints, and colic, as well as to soothe sunburn, repel insects, fight infection, guard against disease, and relieve pain. (In 17th-century London, a bunch of lavender worn around the wrist was said to ward off the plague.)

In addition, lavender has long been considered to have relaxing qualities and is frequently used as a soothing ingredient in cosmetics and natural beauty products. It is said to help induce sleep and it is known especially for its ability to relieve headaches. When added to the bath or used to make facial products, lavender is said to stimulate and cleanse the skin.

Perhaps because Queen Victoria was very enthusiastic about the herb, lavender has been associated with the Victorians. In the Middle Ages, though, even before lavender became the darling of Victorian ladies, the flower was thought to be the herb of love. It is still a popular addition to wedding florals.

Lavender's gray-green leaves are narrow and its small flowers are clustered in spikes. Though it is known for its purple blooms, there are also blue, pink, and white varieties. Lavender is available in floral shops, health food stores, by mail order, or you can grow your own. Lavender requires a sunny spot with very well-drained soil. Dry the flowers by hanging them in small bunches.

Fruit-Scented Soap Balls

⁂

If you want to try your hand at soapmaking, but you're not quite ready to make soap from scratch, soap balls are an easy alternative. This recipe can be made even with leftover soap scraps.

You Will Need

12 ounces (340 g) unscented, uncolored soap, grated into pieces

8 ounces (226 g) water

2 ounces (57 g) fruit fragrance oil, strawberry, orange or any other fragrance of your choice

Several drops of nontoxic dye, such as candle dye, to match the color of the fruit

Heavy stainless steel saucepan

Eyedropper (optional)

Freezer paper

Stainless steel bowl

Rubber gloves (optional)

Instructions

Grate or grind the soap bars into slivers or pieces. You can either grate them by hand on a standard cheese grater (which is effective, but slow) or use an electric grater, which is faster and creates uniformly sized pieces. Add the water to 12 ounces (340 g) of the grated soap pieces and place them together in a heavy, stainless steel saucepan over a low heat. Stir to moisten and allow the soap pieces to melt together until they form a paste. Next, remove the soap from the heat and add dye, a very small amount at a time, until the desired level of color is achieved. Add the fragrance oil in the same manner. (Using an eyedropper for this process will prevent costly spills.)

Place the soap in a plastic container and set aside to harden. (Putting this container in the freezer will speed up this process.) When the soap is hard, remove the container from the freezer and allow to thaw. When the soap can be cut, slice into uniform blocks that can be held easily in your hand or that can be held in a cheese grater. Place these blocks on freezer paper and allow them to dry out for about one week.

When the blocks are dry, grate as before, placing the grated soap in a stainless steel bowl as you work. Add only enough water to moisten the pieces, and stir the soap until all the pieces are moistened. Any extra water can be drained off.

For the last step, you may wish to wear rubber gloves. Grab a fist full of soap and turn the soap in your hands, using gentle pressure to form a nice hard ball. Continue to squeeze and shape the remaining grated soap to form balls. Dry them on freezer paper, turning them occasionally so that they dry evenly. The soap will need to dry for about two weeks.

Design: Norma Coney

Japanese-Style Body Powder

This powder, similar to the one used by Japanese geisha girls, is scented with essential oils in the exotic fragrances of the Orient. It can be dusted on the body or, if the essential oils are left out, used as a finishing face powder. An antique tin, decorative box, or widowed salt shaker makes a splendid container.

You Will Need

¼ cup (40 g) white rice flour

¼ cup (32 g) arrowroot powder

A few drops essential oil: jasmine, tea rose, green tea extract, or any other oil of your choice (optional)

Instructions

Mix ingredients together evenly with a hand sieve that you use for sifting flour. It will takes several siftings to get the essential oil distributed evenly. (Be sure to wash the sifter thoroughly when you are finished.) Give the powder with a powder puff or a large cosmetic brush. The shelf life is about one year.

Design: Casey Kellar

For additional recipes and information on natural cosmetics, see Kellar's book, The Natural Bath & Beauty Book *(Lark, 1997).*

Rosewater

True rosewater is a byproduct of the distillation of roses, but it is easy to achieve similar results in your kitchen. This recipe gives instructions for making rosewater by infusing rose petals. The vodka makes the scented water last longer. An even simpler technique is to add rose essential oil to distilled water.

You Will Need

8 cups (113 g) fresh rose petals

2½ cups (600 ml) distilled water

⅓ cup (80 ml) vodka

Covered saucepan

Strainer

Sterilized glass container

Instructions

Combine the rose petals and the water in a covered saucepan and bring slowly to a boil. Once an active boil is reached, turn down the heat and simmer for several hours. Then remove from heat and allow to sit for two days. After two days, bring the water to a boil once again, then simmer for an hour and a half. Set aside to cool.

Pour the vodka into the bottle or container. Pour water through a nonmetallic strainer into a separate bowl, pressing the rose petals against the strainer. Pour rose infusion into bottle. This recipe makes about 3 cups (720 ml) of rosewater. You can add rose petals to the water for decoration, but tell the recipient to strain out the rosewater into another container before use.

🌿 Design: Laura Dover Doran

Powder Puff

Cross-stitch fabric is perfect for holding fragrant body powder inside, while also allowing it to come out when "puffed." This clever design is simple and the powder can be replenished easily as needed.

You Will Need

For the powder

1 cup (28 g) lavender flowers

1 cup (28 g) dried rose petals or buds

1 tablespoon powdered benzoin gum

1 teaspoon essential oil of lavender or rose geranium or a blend of the two

2 cups (250 g) cornstarch

Food processor or blender

Small bowl

Sealed bag or container

For the puff

14-inch (35.5-cm) square of large-count cross-stitch fabric

18 inches (45.5 cm) tapestry ribbon

18 inches (45.5 cm) satin cording

Polyester filling

Rubber band

For the puff holder

5-inch (12.5-cm) terra-cotta saucer

Spray paint, white

Instructions

To make the powder: Whirl lavender flowers in a food processor until they are reduced to a powder. Repeat this process with the dried rose petals. Combine the powdered lavender and roses, the cornstarch, and the

benzoin gum (available at drug stores) in food processor or blender and mix until thoroughly blended. Pour mixture into a small bowl and stir in the essential oils. Set mixture aside in a sealed bag or container for three days to allow the oils to penetrate the powder.

For the puff, stitch 1 inch (2.5 cm) around the outside edges of the square piece of cross-stitch fabric. Fringe all outside edges up to the line of stitching by pulling the threads out. Place about a cup of the powder in the center of the square and top off with polyester filling. Gather up the four corners and all edges and secure with a rubber band. Wrap tapestry ribbon and satin cording around puff to cover rubber band and tie in a bow or decorative knot. Tie knots in each end of cording.

Spray-paint the saucer white, then set aside to dry thoroughly. Place the remaining powder in a decorative tin or container, and place puff on the saucer. The recipient can replenish the powder in the puff as needed.

🌿 Design: Kim Tibbals-Thompson

Sandalwood Foot Rub

Is there anything more luxurious than a foot massage? Encourage those you love to be kind to themselves by treating them to this moisturizing foot rub.

You Will Need

½ cup (120 ml) almond oil

¼ cup (60 ml) apricot kernel oil

1 tablespoon cocoa butter

2 tablespoons beeswax

10 drops sandalwood essential oil or any other oil of your choice

Heat-safe glass or ceramic bowl

Small saucepan

Instructions

Combine the almond oil, apricot kernel oil, cocoa butter, and beeswax in a small, nonmetallic container (a glass measuring cup works well) and place in a saucepan that has about 2 inches (5 cm) of water in it. Heat the mixture over medium heat until the beeswax has melted completely. Remove from heat, and, as it cools slightly, add the essential oil. Pour into containers and set aside to cool. Makes about 1 cup of foot rub. Note: wax is flammable; heat gently and never leave melting wax unattended.

❧ Design: Kelly Davis

Peppermint Lip Balm

Peppermint essential oil gives this balm a tingly mint sensation, but you can substitute any essential oil of your choosing. Vitamin E is a healing agent and also acts as a preservative.

You Will Need

2 tablespoons almond, sunflower, or safflower oil

1 tablespoon beeswax

2 vitamin E capsules

2 drops peppermint essential oil

Heat-safe glass or ceramic bowl

Small saucepan

Instructions

Make the lip balm the same way you would the foot rub (see page 54), by combining the oil, beeswax, and vitamin E in a makeshift double-boiler setup over medium heat and adding essential oil just before you pour the mixture into containers. This makes two ½-ounce (14-g) tins of lip balm.

🌿 Design: Kelly Davis

Presentation

You probably know and envy someone who presents gorgeous packages on every occasion. No matter how wonderful your gift, if it is not presented attractively, you're depriving the recipient of part of the pleasure. Here are a few practical tips that may make your gifts the object of someone else's envy.

If at all possible, wrap or enclose your gift in some way. Most people enjoy ripping through paper, ribbon, and stuffing to get to their gift. Resist the urge to use commercially made wrapping paper; it is expensive, and a package that you've taken the time to put together yourself holds a special significance. That being said, don't allow your package to outshine your gift—often the most simple presentations are the most effective. Even brown shipping paper can be recycled as wrapping paper—dress it up with a piece of raffia or ribbon. Fabric wrapping also works well.

If your gift consists of several small items, wrap them separately—it prolongs the anticipation. If you are giving an accessory gift (a corkscrew with wine, batteries with toys, seed packets with gardening gloves, and so forth), attach it to the larger package in some creative fashion.

If wrapping is not your forté, try to choose a container that can stand alone. Baskets are a perfect container for a variety of gifts and are also useful. Pick a container that is related in some way to the gift—a watering can, toolbox, or flowerpot, for example.

🌿 Always have supplies on hand. Nothing is more frustrating than rushing around at the last minute to find the appropriate wrap or ribbon. Keeping a basket filled with scraps and tools will surely take off some of the gift-giving pressure. Just rummaging through your stash is sure to get your creative juices flowing.

🌿 Give the recipient instructions on how to best use the gift. If your gift is a homemade food item, neatly copy the recipe onto a recipe card and attach to the package.

🌿 Skin care products are appealing when packaged in antique tins, pretty glass bottles, or any other specialty container. (Make sure you clean them thoroughly.) Include self-adhesive labels describing the product, the ingredients, and instructions for use.

🌿 Beyond the actual packaging, consider how, when, and where you want to present the gift. Gifts have more impact when the circumstances of giving are planned carefully.

🌿 Put some thought into the gift tag. A handmade tag not only personalizes the gift, but can add to its aesthetic value (see page 58). Save potential gift tag items; I have a box of collected bits of paper and fabric for this purpose. Consider creating a tag that can be saved and used, such as a Christmas ornament or bookmark. Edible tags—cookies, lollipops, fortune cookies, and so forth—are always a hit.

Pressed Flower and Herb Gift Cards

❧❀❧

Pressed flower gift tags are the perfect accompaniment to scented gifts,
and, with a drop of essential oil, you can scent them, too.

You Will Need

Assorted flowers, foliage, and herbs

Blotting paper

Flower press or heavy book

Handmade or decorative paper note cards

Medium matte acrylic, white craft glue,
or clear contact paper

Assorted ribbon or raffia, approximately
3 to 6 inches (7.5 to 15 cm) per tag or card

Scissors

Hole punch

Instructions

Choose plants that will dry well and press nicely; flatter plants work best. If you have a flower press, position the plant between sheets of blotter paper and put sheets in the press; you can also place flowers between the pages of a large book. The flowers should be ready in two to three weeks. See page 19 for more information on pressing flowers.

Plant material can be attached to the handmade paper and note cards with medium matte acrylic, white craft glue, or clear contact paper. Here, acrylic was used: it was applied to the paper surface before the flowers were arranged on the sheet, then a second coat of acrylic was applied over the flowers to seal them to the paper surface. (If applied smoothly, acrylic medium does not show when dry.) Since many dried leaves and petals are very delicate, use a soft brush to apply the glue to avoid damaging the plant.

Embellish tags with small pieces of thin satin ribbon or with raffia ties. Use a hole punch to make openings for the ribbon. Colored pencils and watercolors can also be used to add details to individual petals or to create borders on cards.

❦ Design: Barbara Morgan

Gifts
from the
Kitchen

Whether it's
a sweetly scented
cake still warm
from the oven
or a jar of home-
made mint jelly,
folks have been
exchanging food
gifts as a gesture
of friendship and
affection for cen-
turies. Perhaps
this is because
nothing can
quite replace
the flavor and
aroma of home-
made edibles.

Gingerbread

Surely nothing is as comforting as the warm, cozy smell of gingerbread baking in the oven. A festively packaged loaf makes a perfect hostess gift for a holiday gathering.

You Will Need

2¼ cups (155 g) all-purpose flour

1½ teaspoons powdered ginger

1¼ teaspoons powdered cinnamon

½ teaspoon cloves

½ teaspoon nutmeg

½ teaspoon salt

2 teaspoons baking powder

2 eggs

¾ cup (100 g) brown sugar, sifted

¾ cup (250 g) molasses

¾ cup (145 g) shortening, melted

½ teaspoon soda

1 cup (240 ml) boiling water

Loaf pan, 9 x 5 x 3 inches (23 x 12.5 x 7.5 cm)

Large saucepan

Electric rotary beater

Wooden spoon

Plastic wrap (optional)

Sterilized cheesecloth or gauze and ribbon (optional)

Instructions

Preheat oven to 350° F (180° C). Grease the bottom and sides of the pan, then line the pan with wax paper. Grease the wax paper. Sift flour separately, then add the ginger, cinnamon, cloves, nutmeg, salt, and baking powder. Sift three more times.

Beat eggs in large saucepan with an electric beater. Beat in sifted brown sugar, molasses, and shortening. When the mixture is very creamy, clean off and remove beaters, and beat with wooden spoon. Stir in flour mixture in two portions until well mixed. Add soda dissolved in boiling water. Beat again with electric beater until well mixed.

Pour into prepared pans and bake for 35 minutes. Cool on baking rack for five minutes, then turn cake out of pan and strip off wax paper carefully. Before giving, wrap in plastic wrap, then in sterilized gauze or cheesecloth. Tie with a ribbon and attach a label. Makes one loaf.

❦ Design: Georgia Shuford

Herbal Cooking Oils

❧✤❧

Oils flavored with your favorite herbs from the garden can be substituted for regular cooking oils in virtually any dish. They are especially marvelous when used for sautéing vegetables and as dipping oils for fresh bread.

You Will Need

Assorted fresh herbs: basil, chives, cilantro, rosemary, thyme, and/or sage

High-quality cooking oil, approximately as much as the volume of the bottles

Decorative bottles with lids

Clay tags and ribbon (see instructions, right) or other labels

Instructions

To make the oils, pour cooking oil into the bottles until the bottles are about two-thirds full. Place the desired herbs in each bottle and top off with oil. (Chopsticks are useful for placing the herbs.) Herbal cooking oils last only about three weeks, so make sure you tell the recipient to use it right away or only for decorative purposes. Gifts of small containers of oil help to keep it from going to waste

Since unglazed clay accepts and retains scented oils, these clay tags make attractive and fragrant labels. They can be washed in the dishwasher or by hand, so they are reusable. You can purchase red clay from any local ceramics or craft supply store and can also have your pieces fired there for a minimal fee (see page 110 for more information and other fragrant clay projects). Using a sharp knife, cut the clay into triangles and press them against the bottle so that they will fit nicely when fired. Make sure you make holes for the ribbon *before* you take the labels to be fired. Once fired, use a permanent pen or marker to identify the oils, then add a few drops of the herbal oil to the clay for a wonderfully fragrant gift tag.

🌿 Design: Kirsten Jasna

Delicious preserved lemons, herbal tea, and an aromatic simmer are all delectable fragrant treats that can be prepared ahead of time and stored for use as last-minute gifts. (See pages 66-67 for instructions.)

Preserved Lemons

These preserved lemons are as useful as they are decorative. Water-packed lemons can be used for any recipe that calls for fresh lemon, including lemonade, salad dressing, and garnishes. The oil-packed version makes a nice flavoring in a variety of dishes, and the oil can be used when its lovely, lemony flavor is appropriate. Oil-packed lemons are particularly good in stuffing.

You Will Need

Lemons

Coarse salt or kosher salt

Sterilized jars

Olive oil or distilled spring water

Instructions

Cut lemons into slices or wedges. Sprinkle each lemon piece with coarse salt or kosher salt. Place lemons in sterilized jars, fill with olive oil or distilled water, and cover tightly. Let stand in a warm spot for three to four weeks, then store in the refrigerator. Lemons will keep for several months. Note: The water-packed lemons will need to be rinsed thoroughly before they are eaten.

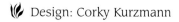 Design: Corky Kurzmann

Warming Solace Tea

This herbal tea will take the nip out of even the coldest winter day—and cheer a friend who is under the weather. Candied ginger is known for its warming properties as well as its ability to calm an upset stomach. Dried lemon peel gives the mixture a wonderful smell and helps to lift the spirits.

You Will Need

2 cups (32 g) dried spearmint

¾ cup (50 g) dried lemon peel

2 tablespoons finely diced candied ginger root

½ cup (50 g) cloves

1 tablespoon cardamom seeds

1 tablespoon anise seeds

Glass container (at least 1 gallon or 3.8 l) with tight-fitting lid

Instructions

Mix herbs and spices together in a large jar or container and seal with a lid. Attach label that includes the following instructions for using the tea: Place 1 heaping teaspoon of the herbal tea for each person plus an extra teaspoon "for the pot" into a teapot that has been prewarmed with boiling water. Pour in 1 cup (240 ml) boiling water per cup of tea and steep for five minutes. Strain into teacups and sweeten, either with honey or sugar. In summer, add ice to a strong brew for a refreshing iced tea.

 Design: Alyce Nadeau

Nostalgia Simmer

The woodsy, spicy scents associated with the holiday season seem to bring out sentimentality in even the most reluctant seasonal scrooge. When this mixture of spices is left simmering on the stove top, your guests will know a festive occasion is at hand. Send them home with an attractively packaged jar of the simmer and a copy of the recipe.

You Will Need

3 cups (200 g)
dried lemon pieces

3 cups (290 g) cloves

3 cups (200 g)
dried orange peel

1½ cups (145 g)
sassafras root pieces

3 cups (125 g) star anise

15 tonka beans, split
lengthwise and chopped in small pieces

3 cups (325 g) cinnamon sticks, broken
into 1-inch (2.5-cm) lengths

1 cup (100 g) cardamom pieces

4 cups (60 g) chopped
or finely cut bay leaves

3 cups (350 g) balsam needles

3 tablespoons orris root, chopped into
granules and soaked in tangerine oil

Large, nonmetal container
or brown paper bag

Wooden spoon with long handle

Instructions

To make this simmer, simply combine the above ingredients in a nonmetal container or a brown paper bag; a metal container will cause the oils to become rancid over time. Package your simmer in a pretty glass bowl and provide the recipient with the following instructions: Place mixture in a simmer pot or saucepan on stove (preferably a wood stove) with just enough water to cover the mix. Bring to a boil, then reduce the heat and simmer. Be careful not to allow the pot to dry out.

Note: While sassafras root is perfectly safe for external use, it is toxic when taken internally.

 Design: Alyce Nadeau

Savory Herb Jelly

This jelly, rich with the flavors and scents of freshly gathered herbs, is a pleasure for the nose as well as the palate. Experiment with various mixtures of herbs—you'll be surprised at how wonderful (and different) each will be. This jelly is superb on crackers with cream cheese.

You Will Need

¼ cup (12 g) dry or 1½ cups (60 g) fresh, crushed herbs

2½ cups (600 ml) water

3½ cups (700 g) granulated sugar

¼ cup (60 ml) distilled white vinegar

1 tablespoon lemon juice

½ package liquid pectin

Medium saucepan

Large saucepan

Instructions

First, select any combination of leafy herbs to make the herb infusion; oregano, basil, thyme, marjoram, tarragon, and mint work well. Measure the dry or fresh herbs into a medium saucepan. Pour 2½ cups (600 ml) of boiling water over the herbs, place the lid on the pan, and allow the herbs to steep for one hour. Then strain out the leaves and reserve the liquid.

In a large saucepan, combine 1¾ cups (420 ml) of the herb infusion with the sugar, vinegar, and lemon juice. Bring to a vigorous boil over high heat, stirring constantly. Add the liquid pectin, return to a boil, and boil vigorously for one minute. Remove the pan from the heat, skim away any foam, and ladle into sterilized jars, leaving ¼ inch (.5 cm) headspace. Process for five minutes in a boiling-water bath. Yields three half-pints.

Refreshing Mint Jelly

If you have mint, you probably have lots of mint, since mint plants are hardy and tend to spread quickly (see page 70). However, this hardiness is a virtue rather than a vice, because mint is a versatile herb that can be put to good use in hundreds of ways. Mint jelly is one of my favorites. It is traditionally served with meat (particularly lamb), but is a delicious accompaniment to a variety of dishes.

You Will Need

4 cups (960 ml) extracted apple juice (4 pounds or 12 medium apples)

1¼ cups (27 g) packed mint leaves

1 cup (240 ml) boiling water

1 tablespoon lemon juice

1 tablespoon lime juice

3 cups (600 g) sugar

Green food coloring (optional)

Large saucepan

Medium saucepan

Colander

Sterilized gauze

Instructions

First, you will need to extract the apple juice. One-fourth of your apples should be underripe, the rest fully ripe. Wash the fruit thoroughly in cold running water. Crush the apples if they are soft; cut them into pieces if they are firm. Don't bother to peel or core the fruit, since much of the pectin you're after is in these parts of the fruit.

Place the fruit in a large saucepan. If the apples are firm, cover them with water; if they are soft, add only enough water to keep them from scorching. Bring the fruit and water to a gentle simmer over low heat, stirring constantly. Soft fruits will need about 10 minutes of simmering, and firm fruits about 20 to 30 minutes. Pour the cooked fruit and liquid into a colander lined with several pieces of sterilized gauze that has been placed over a broad-mouthed pan or medium saucepan. Allow the juice to drain into the pan; do not squeeze the bag, or your jelly will be cloudy.

Make a mint infusion by placing the mint leaves in a saucepan and covering them with 1 cup (240 ml) of boiling water. Place a lid on the pan and allow the mint leaves to steep for at least one hour. Strain the leaves from the liquid.

In a large saucepan, combine the apple, lemon, and lime juices with ½ cup (120 ml) of the mint infusion. Bring to a boil over high heat, then add the sugar. Bring the mixture back to a vigorous boil, stirring to dissolve the sugar, and cook to the jellying point. Skim away any foam, stir in the food coloring, and ladle the jelly into sterilized jars, leaving ¼ inch (.5 cm) headspace. Process for five minutes in a boiling-water bath. Yields four half-pints.

 Design: Georgia Shuford

MINT

Ancient mythology has it that, when Persephone discovered that her husband Pluto was in love with the nymph Minthe, she changed Minthe into a plant. Pluto was unable to reverse the spell but was not to be completely undone, and determined that the more the plant was tread upon, the more fragrant it would become. Sometime thereafter, the name Minthe changed to Menthe, which is the genus name of the herb we know as mint.

Persephone probably did not intend for the lowly plant she created, valued for its cool, refreshing scent, to be among the most common and widely enjoyed herbs. Mint has a bounty of uses—medicinal, culinary, aromatic, ornamental, and cosmetic. Spearmint and peppermint are the most well-known mints, but dozens of other varieties are available, including field mint, pineapple mint, Corsican mint, chocolate mint, ginger mint, bergamot mint, water mint, curly mint, horse mint, pennyroyal, and apple mint.

Mints are distinguished by their square stems and spreading root systems, and prefer rich, moist, well-drained soil in full sun to partial shade. Mint can grow up to two feet high and can be quite invasive—it will take over your herb garden if you're not careful. Therefore, it may need to be confined to a limited space or planted in a bottomless container. Mint flowers in July and August, producing tiny blooms that can be purple, pink, or white. Its delightful fragrance comes from the leaves, which are simple-toothed. It is best and easily propagated by cuttings, layerings, or divisions.

Pineapple Mint

Mint tastes wonderful in combination with a variety of herbs, and can be used in beverages, salads, and soups, as well as with meats, vegetables, and dairy products. The leaves dry well in the microwave. Place the fresh mint between two paper towels and microwave on high for three to four minutes, or until crisp and completely dry. You can also hang them in bunches to dry or freeze them in plastic bags. See page 18 for more information on drying herbs and flowers.

Herb Salts

This seasoning mix is free of chemicals (provided you know the herbs are organically grown) and is a healthy and tasty alternative to iodized salt. A shaker full of this delightful herb blend and a copy of the recipe is certain to be a much-appreciated gift.

You Will Need

½ cup mixed, fresh, organically grown herbs or 8 tablespoons each of rosemary, chives, tarragon, thyme, oregano, basil, garlic, and dill

½ cup (160 g) sea salt

Clean jars or other containers

Mortar and pestle or blender

Cookie sheet

Instructions

Do not wash the herbs unless it is necessary, because any residual moisture will cause the herb salt to clump. First, mix the fresh herbs together with the sea salt. When thoroughly mixed, mince the herbs and salt together, using a mortar and pestle or a blender.

After blending, spread salt mixture on a cookie sheet and cook in a 200° F (90° C) oven for about 40 to 50 minutes, or until the mixture seems dry. Be sure to break up any lumps and stir frequently while drying. When cool, pour into a glass jar and seal. *Variation:* add paprika for a lovely color.

🌿 Design: Corky Kurzmann

Pesto

❧❀❧

Pesto is an herb paste that is traditionally made with fresh basil and tossed with pasta, though it has become more and more common to see pestos made from oregano, dill, and a variety of unusual herbs. And far from being used exclusively with pasta, this savory mixture is magnificent with chicken, fish, vegetables, and even on pizza.

You Will Need

2 cups (80 g) fresh basil leaves

¼ cup (40 g) pine nuts

½ cup (120 ml) olive oil

2 cloves garlic

⅓ cup (25 g) grated
fresh Parmesan cheese

Blender or food processor

Instructions

Place all of the ingredients in a blender or a food processor and blend until the desired consistency is achieved. Pesto has a very strong flavor and should be used according to taste, as little or as much as desired.

Experiment with different herbs in your pesto. This designer also uses sweet basil, lemon basil, lemon balm, and lemon thyme together to make a delicious lemon-flavored pesto that is great with pasta and chicken. Also try almonds and sunflower seeds in place of pine nuts. For a dairy-free recipe, substitute tofu, lemon juice, and salt for the Parmesan cheese.

Pesto freezes nicely in half-pint mason jars and will last for months. Drizzle a few drops of olive oil over the pesto before freezing. Pesto can also be frozen in ice cube trays and then put in freezer bags. Use the pesto cubes in soups or for a quick pasta sauce.

🌿 Design: Corky Kurzmann

Herb Butter Seasoning

This tasty herb butter is great tossed with pastas; on breads, potatoes, and vegetables; or as a baste for fish and poultry. Your friends will be delighted to receive the seasoning, the already-prepared butter, or both.

You Will Need

Dried herbs, equal portions of chives, dill, parsley, basil, marjoram, thyme, lemon balm, and granulated onions

Glass jar or other airtight container

Embellishments for jar (optional)

Instructions

Seasoning that is made of one tablespoon of each herb (listed above) yields about ½ cup (24 g). If you are planning to give just the seasoning, simply mix the ingredients together thoroughly and put in an airtight container. Embellish container with fabric and ribbon, if desired. The mix should be stored out of direct sunlight.

If you are not going to make the butter, you should include instructions for doing so with your gift. Use 2 teaspoons of dried mix per ½ cup or 1 stick (115 g) of butter or margarine. Beat well and refrigerate overnight.

❧ Design: Kathleen Gips

Rosemary-Orange Pound Cake

Before this scrumptious cake makes it to its recipient, it will fill your home with the delightful scents of mingled citrus and rosemary.

You Will Need

For the cake

½ pound (230 g) unsalted butter

1 cup (240 g) sour cream

3 cups (600 g) granulated sugar

6 eggs

1 teaspoon orange extract

1 heaping tablespoon grated dried orange zest

2 teaspoons dried rosemary needles

3 cups (375 g) all-purpose flour

¼ teaspoon salt

¾ teaspoon double-acting baking powder

Cake pan

Large mixing bowl

Wax paper

Vegetable oil

For the glaze

¼ cup (60 ml) fresh orange juice

1 tablespoon Grand Marnier

1 tablespoon grated orange zest, fresh or dried

2 cups (400 g) confectioners' sugar, sifted

Small mixing bowl

For the garnish (optional)

Orange slices

Sprigs of fresh rosemary

Instructions

Preheat the oven to 350° F (180° C). Spray a cake pan with vegetable oil, line the greased pan with wax paper, then spray the outside of the paper.

Bring all the ingredients for the cake to room temperature. In a large bowl, mix together the ingredients in the order given, adding the eggs one at a time and sifting dry ingredients before mixing them in. Spoon the cake into the greased pan. Bake in the preheated oven for 60 to 75 minutes. Remove cake from oven and place on cooling rack for an hour.

While the cake is cooling, make the glaze. Sift powdered sugar into a small bowl and whisk in other ingredients. Blend until smooth. Invert cake onto cake plate and spread glaze on cake, allowing some glaze to dribble down the sides. Add garnish, if desired.

🌿 Design: Alyce Nadeau

(See page 33 for information on making the citrus pomanders pictured at left.)

Scented Geraniums

Although scented geraniums have been grown and collected since the 17th century and were especially fashionable among Victorian ladies (who ruffled the leaves to emit a fresh scent before guests arrived), they are enjoying increased popularity today. Perhaps this is because they are easy to cultivate and are available in an amazing array of plant shapes, colors, textures, and fragrances. Depending on your preference, choose from cultivars with a variety of evocative scents, ranging from fruity to woody: rose, ginger, lemon-rose, lime, peach, apricot, apple, orange, strawberry, lemon, coconut, chocolate mint, pine, eucalyptus, nutmeg, and peppermint are just a few of the hundreds of scents available.

The plant's foliage provides the scent; beads of oil are contained in the glands at the base of the leaf hairs. Since rubbing the leaf releases the scent, these plants are at their best when placed where there is the highest likelihood that they will be brushed. The leaves are edible and can be used fresh as a flavoring in cakes, jellies, teas, herbal butters, ice cream, and punches (see page 75 for a delicious scented geranium cake recipe). Add chopped geranium leaves to a cup of salad oil, let stand for several hours, and you will have a delicious oil to serve with bread, pasta, or cooked vegetables. The chopped leaves also add a refreshing twist to fresh fruit salads.

What we call scented geraniums are not actually of the genus *geranium*, but rather *pelargonium*. (The same is true of the common garden variety widely available in garden stores—also widely known as geraniums.) Scented geraniums are native to South Africa, where they are grown as perennials. They make great houseplants, are wonderful outdoor plants in the summer (and all year in frost-free regions), and are rarely bothered by insects or disease. They require good air circulation and should not be overwatered. (Also keep in mind that overfertilizing will reduce their scent.)

Cuttings grow quickly and flowers usually appear within three months of rooting. Depending on the variety, the plants reach 1 to 3 feet (.3 to .9 m) tall, and bear small clusters of blooms in summer. To dry leaves to use in potpourris and sachets, pick leaves throughout the summer and store in an airtight container, or dry them on screens or in the microwave (see page 18 for more information on drying herbs and flowers).

You Will Need

For the cake

¾ cup (175 g) unsalted butter, softened

¾ cup (90 g) super-fine sugar

3 eggs, slightly beaten

1½ cups (155 g) self-rising flour, sifted

½ teaspoon vanilla

2 tablespoons milk

Rose geranium leaves

8-inch (20.5-cm) cake pan

Wax paper

For the glaze

½ cup (60 g) confectioners' sugar, sifted

½ teaspoon water

Scented Geranium Cake

Scented geranium leaves work well in a host of culinary creations because they impart a delicious flavor as well as a distinctive scent. Simply lining a cake pan with the leaves distributes the pleasantly sweet flavor through the batter as the cake cooks. We've used rose geranium leaves for this cake, but feel free to use any scented geranium variety you have handy.

Instructions

Preheat oven to 350° F (180° C). Lightly grease and flour the cake pan. Cream together butter and sugar thoroughly until light and creamy. Add eggs, one at a time, beating thoroughly between each egg, until mixture is thick and glossy. Fold in flour, vanilla, and milk. Line the pan with wax paper and place rose geranium leaves on the side of the pan. Carefully spoon mixture into pan and bake approximately one hour. Allow to set for five minutes, then remove from pan to cool.

To make the glaze, mix the confectioners' sugar and water and dribble over cake. You can also use rosewater in place of the water for the glaze—it gives the cake extra rose scent and flavor. For a variation that makes a nice afternoon tea cake, add 1 teaspoon finely chopped lavender flowers to the cake batter and use lavender water for the icing.

 Design: Corky Kurzmann

Herbal Vinegars

❧❀❧

Herbal vinegars are quite expensive in gourmet food stores, but are remarkably easy and economical to make at home. They make very attractive gift items. Let the recipient know (possibly on the gift tag) the ingredients and that the vinegar should not be stored in direct sunlight. There are a number of ways to make herbal vinegars. Here are three common methods.

Traditional Heating Method

The conventional method of making herbal vinegars uses heat—either from the sun or the stove top—to extract the maximum flavor and scent from the herbs.

You Will Need

12-ounce (340-g) sterilized bottles with corks

White vinegar, white wine vinegar

Assorted fresh herbs

Paraffin wax or beeswax (optional)

Double-boiler setup (optional)

Ribbons, raffia, or other embellishments (optional)

Instructions

Heat 1 gallon (4.5 l) of white vinegar: Either combine the ingredients in a pot over low heat (do not boil) for 15 to 20 minutes, or heat the mixture in the sun in a 1-gallon (4.5-l) jug for a couple of hours. *Note:* If you choose to cook the vinegar, do not use metallic cookware or utensils, as it will influence the flavor. Put two to three handfuls of fresh, clean herbs in a 1-gallon (4.5-l) jug and add the heated vinegar. Cover the container and place it in a dark, cool place. Let the herbs steep for four to six weeks.

Once the herbs have steeped, strain the mixture, separating the herbs from the liquid. (Many herbs, such as nasturtiums, will break up considerably.) Place several rinsed, fresh herb sprigs in each bottle (it does not necessarily need to be the herbs you used to steep the vinegar), add 3 tablespoons of white wine vinegar, and fill each bottle with the white vinegar infusion. Cork the bottles.

Sealing the bottles with wax is optional. Heat paraffin or beeswax in a double boiler over low heat. (Any adapted double-boiler setup will work just as well.) Be careful not to overheat the wax, as it is highly flammable. You can add pieces of colored crayons to color the wax. Dip the tops of the bottles in the hot wax several times to seal. Embellish the bottles as desired. Add label.

Nasturtium-Tarragon Vinegar (#1): Contains nasturtiums and tarragon. This vinegar is best used for salad dressing—with or without oil. You can also make it with tarragon or purple basil alone, which makes a delicious marinade.

Basil Vinegar (#4): Contains lemon, sweet cinnamon, and purple basil. Good with tomato dishes, beef, or liver; also marvelous on pasta or as a salad dressing.

Mint and Anise Hyssop Vinegar (#8): Contains mint and anise hyssop. The blooms of anise hyssop are gorgeous and the scent is divine. This combination is wonderful with green vegetables (peas, green beans, greens), meats, and salads.

🌿 Heated Vinegar Design: Vicki Baker

Microwave Method

Another quick and simple way to make herbal vinegars is to heat them in the microwave, as we have done with the **Mixed-Herb Vinegar** (see **#5**, **#7**, and **#10** in the photo). This aromatic vinegar blend will add pizzazz to tossed salads (mix with olive or walnut oil) or cooked greens. It is also an excellent meat marinade.

You Will Need

Clean glass bottles in assorted sizes

2 cups (480 ml) white vinegar

Coffee filter paper

Assorted fresh herbs

Paraffin wax or beeswax (optional)

Double-boiler setup (optional)

Ribbons, raffia, or other embellishments (optional)

Instructions

For this vinegar, you will need 1 tablespoon peppercorns and 1 teaspoon caraway seeds, as well as an assortment of freshly gathered herbs. Here we've used bay leaves, rosemary, borage blossoms, thyme, lemon verbena, chives, garlic, and banana pepper strips; feel free to do some experimenting to determine what combinations of herbs suits you—the possibilities are endless.

Once you've gathered the herbs, wash them thoroughly and pat them dry. Insert the herbs into clean bottles. A chopstick is a useful tool for positioning the herbs inside the bottle. Add approximately three cloves of garlic and three strips of banana pepper last. (The number will depend on the size of the bottle.)

Heat the white vinegar in a microwave-safe container (it should be at least a 3-cup [720-ml] container) for four minutes. Pour hot vinegar over the herbs into the bottle through a coffee filter. Make sure herbs are covered. Cork or cap, then wash the outside of the bottle. Seal with wax, if you like (see above). Decorate the bottleneck with raffia bow or other embellishment. Add label.

🌿 Microwave Vinegar Design: Alyce Nadeau

Unheated Method

Some gourmets feel that heating the vinegar changes the flavor; they prefer to let flavored vinegars cure on their own without the addition of heat.

You Will Need

Clean glass bottles or jars in assorted sizes

White wine vinegar

Fresh herbs and berries

Paraffin wax or beeswax (optional)

Double-boiler setup (optional)

Ribbons, raffia, or other embellishments (optional)

Instructions

Simply place herbs or berries inside sterilized jars then fill jars to the top with white wine vinegar. A plastic or other nonmetallic funnel is helpful. Cork or close tightly and seal with wax if desired (see page 78). Store in a cool, dark place for at least a month, shaking occasionally.

Raspberry Vinegar (#2 and **#6):** Contains fresh, ripe organic raspberries. Add just enough to cover the bottom of the container (or to taste), then pour in vinegar. Great on fish or salads or as a marinade.

Rosemary and Pansy Vinegar (#9): Add sprigs of rosemary and several pansies. A delightful, low-fat salad dressing.

🔥 Unheated Vinegar Design: Corky Kurzmann

Purple Sage

Sewn
Gifts

Fabric and fragrance have been bedfellows for centuries. When sewing fragrant sachets and pillows, try to choose fabrics made of natural fibers—cotton, muslin, and linen, for example—because these fabrics will not only absorb the scent, but will allow it to escape.

Fragranced Guest Room Pillow

※※◎◎※※

This project is a great way to make use of an antique handkerchief without cutting or damaging the fabric. Sew along the seams of the handkerchief so as not to create an unnecessary seam line. For this pillow, try to match the fabric—sometimes called "hanky linen"—to the handkerchief as closely as possible.

You Will Need

For the pillow insert

2 pieces cotton muslin, each 12 inches (30.5 cm) square

Stuffing material (down feathers, polyester stuffing, and potpourri)

For the envelope pillowcase

1 piece linen, 12 x 30½ inches (30.5 x 77.5 cm)

Linen handkerchief, 11 inches (28 cm) square

1 foot (.3 m) satin ribbon, ½ inch wide (1.5 cm)

1 button

Instructions

First, make a square pillow to go inside the envelope covering: Pin the fabric pieces with right sides together. Sew the two pieces of muslin together with a ½-inch (1.5-cm) seam, leaving a 6-inch (15-cm) opening for the stuffing. Trim and turn the pillow to the right side. Carefully fill the pillow with the stuffing and handstitch the opening closed. (Here, we've used a mixture of down feathers, polyester stuffing, and potpourri, but feel free to substitute your own fragranced stuffing.)

Finish off what will be the inner edge of the envelope pillowcase by either stitching a double ½-inch (1.5-cm) hem or adding a 2-inch (5-cm) facing. Next, fold over 10 inches (25.5 cm) of the fabric with the right sides together and stitch ½-inch (1.5-cm) seams on both sides.

To get a squared-off bottom, fold each corner to a point, centering the seam. Stitch across, exactly perpendicular to the seam line and approximately 1¼ inches (3.5 cm) in from the end of the seam. To finish off the upper flap of the envelope pillow, cut rounded corners and stitch a narrow hem around the flap. Position pillow insert in pillowcase and tuck flap under.

Now that the pillow is complete, it is time to sew on the embellishments. This linen handkerchief is 11 x 11 inches (25.5 x 25.5 cm) with a decorative edging. Lay the handkerchief across the pillow to judge placement; handstitch one edge to the back of the pillowcase. This designer crocheted a loop with embroidery floss, but you can also weave a simple braid or use a ribbon. Tie a bow with the satin ribbon and sew bow on pillow. Place a button so that the loop will fit snugly over it and sew the button in place.

🌿 Design: Tracy Munn

Cloth-Covered Vase

⚘

This adorable little flower container is actually a fabric bag that has been made to fit over an ordinary tin can. Hung on a doorknob or rested against a step, it makes a delightful and reusable vessel for a small bunch of scented flowers. It's a wonderful housewarming gift.

You Will Need

For outside of bag: 1 piece brushed cotton fabric, 6 x 10½ inches (15 x 26.5 cm)

For the inside of bag: 1 piece brushed cotton fabric in a coordinating color, 8 x 10¼ inches (20.5 x 30 cm)

10¾-ounce (305-g) soup can

Raffia or ribbon

Scented bouquet of flowers or herbs

Instructions

Fold the 6- x 10½-inch (15- x 26.5-cm) piece of fabric (the outside piece) in half with the right side of the fabric facing inward. Stitch one long side and one short side together, leaving one short side open. Turn right side out to form the outside bag.

Fold inside fabric in half as well, again with the right side of fabric facing inward. On one short edge, fold and press 2 inches (5 cm) toward the wrong side to form a band at top—the band should be the right side of the fabric. Pin and stitch the long side and the unfolded short side with a ½-inch (1.5-cm) seam. Do not turn this bag inside out.

Slip inside bag into outside bag and roll top down 1 inch (2.5 cm) to create a cuff. Insert tin can into bag. Tie ribbon or raffia around can under cuff. Either tie a bow with the raffia or use raffia to secure vase to a doorknob. Fill with water and freshly cut, scented bouquet.

🌿 Design: Mardi Letson

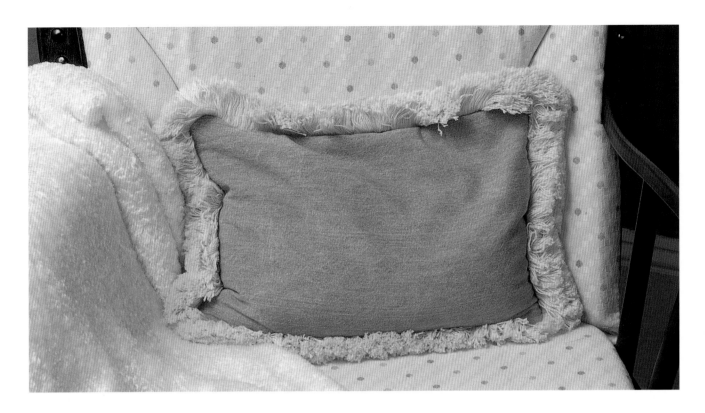

Pregnancy Back Pillow

If you know someone who is expecting a baby, chances are she has an achy back.
This pillow is filled with flaxseed, which makes it conform to and support the lower back.
It's scented with lavender, which is known for its relaxing qualities.

You Will Need

2 pieces of denim, 15 x 11 inches
(38 x 28 cm)

Fringe, about 55 inches (139.5 cm)

Flaxseed

Lavender, dried

Instructions

Pin fringe around the edge of the front of one piece of fabric and baste fringe to the fabric. Remove pins. Place fringed piece of denim against other piece with right sides together and pin. Stitch around the edge, using a seam large enough to cover the welt or binding of the fringe. Leave a 3- to 4-inch (7.5- to 10-cm) opening. Reverse the pillow by pulling it through the opening. Fill the bag with lavender and flaxseed until it is about three-fourths full. The lavender provides the scent; use as much or as little as desired. Handstitch the opening closed.

Design: Mardi Letson

Antique Linen Sachets

Working with antique linens requires that you first find a piece of linen that you like, then plan the sachet. Experiment with folding and positioning linen to determine how best to accentuate embroidery, colors, or fabric.

You Will Need

Assorted antique linens, such as handkerchiefs, napkins, scarfs, or small pieces of tablecloths

Assorted potpourri

Polyester filling

Buttons (optional)

Instructions

For linens with one small area of embroidery, consider a simple fold that will present the design on the outermost flap, as shown in **sachet #6**. First, make an inner pillow with a piece of cotton fabric that is approximately 1 inch (2.5 cm) larger than the size of the linen: stitch the sides together, leaving several inches open; then turn the pillow right side out and stuff with potpourri and polyester filler. Handstitch opening closed. Starch the piece of linen for a stiffer, crisper look. Fold the linen over the inner pillow and either handstitch in place (#6) or secure with a coordinating button (**#2**).

A piece that has a design on the corners works well when the four edges are gathered together and tied with a cord or ribbon as in **sachet #1**. Sew a round

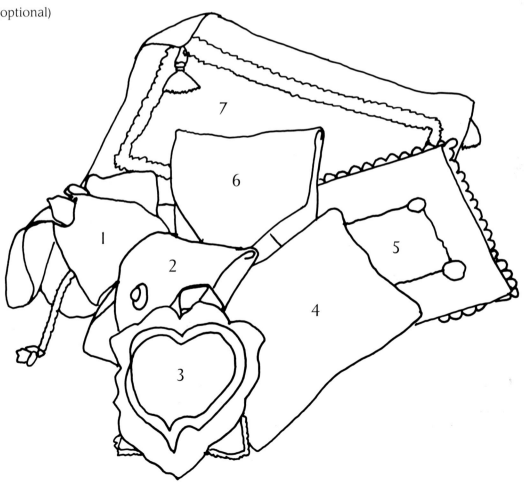

inner pillow following the instructions above, except stitch together two circular pieces instead of a square piece.

A simple pillow can be made from a handkerchief that features an irregular design on one corner, as in **sachet #4**. This is a wonderful way to make use of an antique treasure without having to cut the piece. Fold the handkerchief over with the right side of the embroidery to the inside—the design will fall to one corner of the sachet. Stitch around the edge, leaving several inches (5 cm) open. Turn right side out, stuff with potpourri and polyester filling, and handstitch closed.

 Design: Mardi Letson

Batiste Dream Pillow

This aromatic dream pillow (**#7**) is a prescription for good health and makes a marvelous gift for someone who is feeling ill. It is filled with chamomile, which soothes and encourages sleep and is even said to alleviate colds and coughs.

You Will Need

2 pieces of batiste or other sheer fabric, 13 x 8 inches (33 x 20.5 cm)

1 yard (.9 m) gimp

4 small tassels

Dried chamomile or chamomile-based potpourri

Instructions

Place the two pieces of batiste on top of each other and pin together securely. Stitch a ¼-inch (.5-cm) seam, leaving a 2-inch (5-cm) opening to be used later to insert potpourri. Using small embroidery scissors, cut a precise ⅛-inch (.3-cm) edge around the fabric, leaving an opening.

Turn the pillow right side out. Stitch a square 1 inch (2.5 cm) inside the edge to create the chamber for the potpourri, again leaving a 2-inch (5-cm) opening. Attach gimp to the seam. Remember to leave the 2-inch (5-cm) opening here as well.

Insert potpourri into the pillow. Carefully handstitch all of the open seams closed. Trim the gimp to overlap approximately ½ inch (1.5 cm) and attach remaining gimp. Handstitch tassels to each corner.

 Design: Mardi Letson

Battenberg Lace Sachet

This dainty lace sachet (**#3**) is easily tucked into a lingerie drawer or hung in a linen closet.

You Will Need

2 pieces of linen, each 4 inches (10 cm) square

1 Battenberg lace decoration

4 inches (10 cm) ½ inch wide (1.5 cm) white satin ribbon

14 inches (35.5 cm) tatting

Potpourri

Instructions

Pin the pieces of linen with right sides together. Sew the pieces together with a ¼-inch (.5-cm) seam, leaving one end open for the stuffing. Trim and turn the sachet to the right side. Carefully fill the sachet with the potpourri and slipstitch the opening closed. Handstitch tatting around the edge of the sachet.

Sew a loop of satin ribbon to the top of the piece of Battenburg lace. Handstitch the lace to one side of the sachet, with the ribbon loop at the top. (Try to stitch to the seam of the lace, so the stitching will not be visible from the front.)

Design: Tracy Munn

Buttons and Lace Sachet

The designer used four of her grandmother's mismatched (though cherished) buttons and some antique lace, but you can use any buttons and lace you may have for this simple little sachet (**#5**). Down feathers and a sprinkling of baby powder create a soft, fragrant filling.

You Will Need

2 pieces of cotton muslin, each 4 inches (10 cm) square

Approximately 1 yard (.9 m) 1¾-inch (4.5-cm) lace

4 buttons

Down filling, enough to fill sachet

Baby powder

Instructions

Pin the linen pieces with right sides together. Sew the two pieces of fabric together with a ¼-inch (.5-cm) seam, leaving an entire end open for stuffing. Trim and turn the sachet to the right side. Carefully fill the sachet with the down feathers, shake in baby powder for the fragrance, and slipstitch the opening closed. Baby powder has a surprisingly concentrated scent, so be careful not to overdo it.

Miter the corners of the lace so that they fit together at corners and handstitch the lace to the sachet with embroidery floss about ½ inch (1.5 cm) in from the edge. Sew buttons at each corner.

Design: Tracy Munn

Baby Sachet

A sachet decorated with whimsical buttons is a perfect decoration for the nursery—it can be tucked among clothes in a dresser or hung on the doorknob to serve as a reminder that the room's occupant is sleeping.

You Will Need

2 pieces of solid fabric,
7 x 5 inches (18 x 12.5 cm)

2 pieces of burlap for overlay,
7 x 5 inches (18 x 12.5 cm)

Whimsical or child-oriented buttons

Flaxseed

Potpourri

Approximately 12 inches (30.5 cm)
½-inch (1.5 cm) ribbon

Instructions

Position fabric pieces in a stack in this order: a piece of solid fabric, both pieces of burlap, and another piece of solid fabric. Stitch a ¾-inch (2-cm) seam around the edge, leaving a 3-inch (7.5-cm) opening on the side that will be the top of the sachet cover. Turn sachet inside out.

Fill the sachet with a mixture of flaxseed and potpourri. How much potpourri you use is entirely a matter of how fragrant you want your sachet to be. As you handstitch the opening closed, insert and stitch ribbon in place for the hanger. Attach buttons. (These buttons were attached with ⅛-inch [3-cm] satin ribbon and a tapestry needle.)
Note: keep this sachet out of reach of small children.

 Design: Mardi Letson

Great Finds

Small treasures found at flea markets, thrift shops, and antique stores can inspire some of the best gift ideas. Vintage linens (tablecloths, hand towels, handkerchiefs, and bed linens) are available in abundance at these haunts, often for very little money, and provide high-quality and unusual fabrics for an endless number of charming sewed gifts: pillows, sachets, neck bolsters, eye pillows, and so forth. And antique beads and buttons make superb accents and embellishments.

Try presenting your gift in a vintage container. An antique tin, after it has been thoroughly cleaned, is the perfect accompaniment to a scented lip balm; if you include the recipe, the recipient can replenish the balm, using the tin you've provided. And don't underestimate the power of a coat of paint or a good scrubbing. An ancient windowsill box with pretty trim will improve immensely with a fresh coat of enamel paint and a few well-placed nails. Keep your eyes peeled for flower pots, glassware, wooden bowls, and garden trugs.

The crocheted gloves pictured here were found by Barbara Morgan, artist and expert antiquer, on one of her regular antiquing jaunts. When stuffed with polyester fiber and spices and laced with pretty satin ribbon, they become inexpensive and easy-to-make sachets.

And odd pieces of charming antique china make for wonderful presentations. A dainty cup and saucer, for example, can temporarily house a cutting or small plant as pictured here. Attach a tea strainer and some herbal tea, and you have a fabulous gift.

Some salvage shops specialize in antique hardware and construction fittings. You can often find a wide range of unusual and inexpensive pieces in these stores and, with a little polishing and some creative presentation, a charming piece of hardware may be the perfect gift for a friend who is renovating an old house. Here, a brass doorknob is an adorable holder for a miniature bouquet.

Housewarming Aprons

An apron isn't likely to inspire a would-be chef, but an apron filled with fragrant herbal teas or dried herbs may do just that. These simple aprons are great gifts for bridal showers or housewarming parties.

You Will Need

For the herbal tea apron: 1 yard (.9 m) 45-inch (114.5-cm) cotton percale

For the pasta herb apron: 1 to 1½ yards (.9 to 1.4 m) eyelet fabric

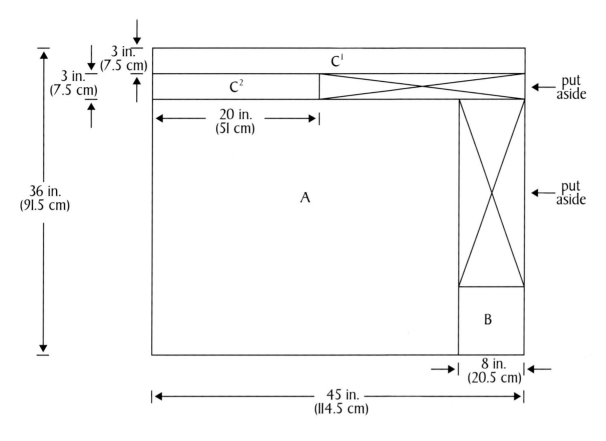

FIG. 1

Instructions

The Basic Apron

First, cut out the fabric as shown in Figure 1. Begin with section A. Fold ¼ inch (.5 cm) back twice around side edges of the fabric, then press and stitch. Make sure you fold away from the front side of the fabric. Fold ¼ inch (.5 cm) at the bottom edge of the fabric, then fold over another 2 inches (5 cm) and stitch. Baste stitch the top edge and pull the thread to gather to 18 to 22 inches (45.5 to 56 cm).

Next, make the front pocket using section B. Fold and press under ¼ inch (.5 cm) on the sides and bottom and 1¼ inch (3 cm) on top. Topstitch seam. Pin to apron and stitch in place as shown in Figure 2.

To make the band, use sections C^1 and C^2. Take section C^1, fold under ¼ inch (.5 cm) twice (toward the back side of the fabric) on all sides of the piece and

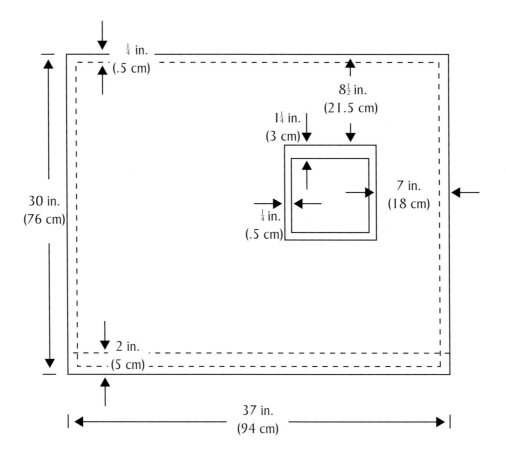

FIG. 2

FIG. 3

Stitch here.

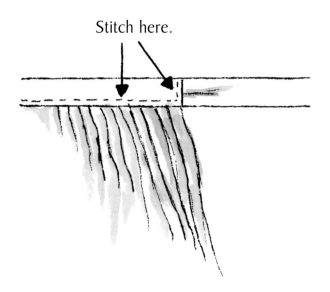

FIG. 4

stitch down. Cut the piece into two equal lengths. Take section C², turn ¼ inch (.5 cm) back on all sides and press. Then press in half along the long side. Fold a pleat on both C¹ pieces along the cut edge to make the pieces fit against C² as shown in Figure 3. Stitch the C¹ pieces to C² with ¼-inch (.5-cm) seams. Place waist band over gathers on apron body. Pin, baste, and stitch sides and bottom of band in place as shown in Figure 4. Follow instructions below for customizing apron.

Herbal Tea Apron (above)

Fill pocket with herbal teas tied in small plastic bags with ribbons in coordinating colors. Include a loose tea strainer.

Herbal Pasta Apron (page 92)

Fill pocket with herbs (basil, bay leaves, and oregano) and an herb-flavored pasta (tomato basil, for example). Include a favorite pasta recipe, if you like.

Variations: A gardening apron with small pots of herbs and seed packets in the pockets or a terry-cloth bath wrap with scented bath salts in the pocket.

🌿 Design: Barbara Morgan

You Will Need

2 pieces of coordinating fabric,
2 x 14 inches (5 x 35.5 cm)

Flaxseed

Potpourri of your choice

Tassels, small (optional)

Instructions

Cut both pieces of fabric in half to create four 6- x 4½-inch (15- x 11.5-cm) pieces. Sew pieces of each fabric together, wrong sides together, with a ¼-inch (.5-cm) seam. Do the same with the remaining two pieces of fabric. You should now have two pieces that measure 4½ x 11½ inches (11.5 x 29 cm) as shown in the illustration below.

Pull hem apart and press flat with an iron. Place pieces together with right sides facing each other and pin around edges. Stitch a ¼-inch (.5-cm) hem around the edge, leaving a 2- to 3-inch (5- to 7.5-cm) opening. Reverse the pillow by pulling it through the opening.

Fill the pillow approximately halfway with a mixture of flaxseed and potpourri. The proportions you use depend on how fragrant you want your eye pillow to be. The potpourri provides the fragrance; the flaxseed gives the pillow its shape. You don't want the pillow to be too full, or it will not conform to the face properly. Handstitch the opening closed and sew tassels to the corners, if desired.

◖ Design: Mardi Letson

Scented Eye Pillows

❧◆❧

You're skeptical? Truly, an eye pillow may be just what a stressed-out friend needs. This easy-to-make version can be elegant or fun, depending on the fabric and the embellishments you choose.

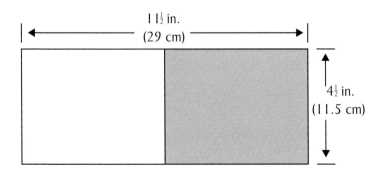

11½ in.
(29 cm)

4½ in.
(11.5 cm)

Checkerboard Hot Pad

Your guests will not forget to save room for dessert if it's waiting on this spice-filled hot pad.

You Will Need

For the patchwork center: twelve 2-inch (5-cm) square pieces of scrap fabric with corresponding designs

For the back side: 12-inch (30.5-cm) square piece of fabric

For the border: two 2- x 8-inch (5- x 20.5-cm) strips of fabric and two 2- x 12-inch (5- x 30.5-cm) strips of fabric

Rice

Cinnamon, powdered

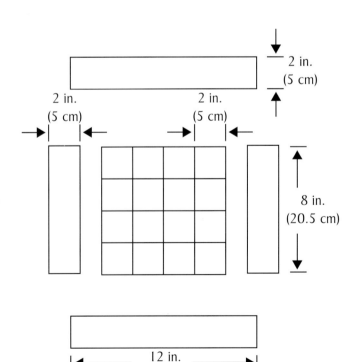

Instructions

Once you have cut the 2-inch (5-cm) square pieces of fabric, lay them out on a flat surface and mix and match squares until you achieve a patchwork design that suits you. Sew squares together to form four strips of four squares, stitching the right sides together with a ¼-inch (.5-cm) seam. Join the four strips to each other.

Choose the border fabric and cut two 2- x 8-inch (5- x 20.5-cm) strips and two 2- x 12-inch (5- x 30.5-cm) strips. First, sew the two shorter pieces to opposite sides, then the two longer pieces to the other two opposite sides.

To make the back side of the pad, cut a 12-inch (30.5-cm) square from the same fabric you used for the border. Lay the front and back sides together with the wrong sides together and topstitch 1 inch (2.5 cm) in from the edge

of the fabric. Stitch along only three sides; leave one side open for the stuffing. Topstitch down the strips of patchwork (to form four channels) and around the outside of the patchwork design; make sure the open side falls on the side of the hot pad that remains unstitched.

Holding the hot pad on its end, carefully stuff the channels that have formed with a mixture of rice and cinnamon powder. Be careful not to overfill the channels. Topstitch along the last edge to close up rice. Use an iron to press under a ¼-inch (.5-cm) seam and topstitch around the entire outer edge of the hot pad.

Design: Tracy Munn

Pet Sachets

Pennyroyal has been used for centuries to repel a variety of household pests. These sachets keep fleas away without chemicals and make a fabulous gift for the friend with a new pet.

You Will Need

1 tablespoon orris root powder

5 drops citronella essential oil

5 drops bay essential oil

20 drops pennyroyal essential oil

1 cup (100 g) dried pennyroyal, crushed

Piece of muslin for each sachet, 7½ x 2¾ inch (19 x 7 cm)

Cotton string

Cardboard

Paint

Paintbrush

Small bowl

Instructions

In a small bowl, mix powdered orris root with the essential oils (citronella, bay, and pennyroyal) until thoroughly blended. Blend in crushed pennyroyal.

Place the piece of muslin in front of you. Fold the short edges over about ¼ inch (.5 cm). Press the folds with an iron and stitch these seams down. Fold the fabric in half with the folded sides facing in and stitch the two long edges closed, with seams about ¼ inch (.5 cm) in from the edges of the fabric.

Turn the bag right side out. At the open end, use a tapestry needle to thread the cotton string through the seam. The string will need to enter the seam, exit and reenter it (in order to bypass the seam on the long edge), and finally exit once again.

Insert a piece of cardboard inside the sachet; this will keep the paint from transferring through to the back piece of fabric. Photocopy the paw print provided and reduce as needed to fit the sachet. Cut out the inside spaces to make a stencil. Position the stencil on the sachet and tape the stencil in place. Paint inside the cutout stencil with acrylic paint, then remove stencil and allow to dry. Once the paint has dried, remove the cardboard, stuff the sachet with the pennyroyal mixture, and pull the drawstring tightly closed. Tie the ends in a double knot to secure the bag's contents.

Instruct the recipient to place the sachets where the animal sleeps. The fragrance will be released when the bag is squeezed or brushed against. These last for up to two years, though the effectiveness of the sachet can be renewed monthly by adding a few drops of pennyroyal essential oil to each bag. (Enclose a container of oil for this purpose, if you wish.) Makes several sachets, depending on how full you stuff them.

🌿 Design: Kathleen Gips

Cedar Sachets

Cedar and lavender are an unusual mixture of fragrances; they actually work wonderfully together. Here are two variations of a cedar-based sachet that the men in your life will adore.

You Will Need

For the drawer sachets

2 pieces fabric, 6 x 25 inches (15 x 63.5 cm) each

2½ feet (.75 m) cording

Rubber band

For the closet sachet

1 piece fabric, 4½ x 19 inches (11.5 x 48.5 cm)

2 feet (.6 m) cording

Rubber band

For the herbal mix

2 cups (30 g) cedar shavings

½ cup (50 g) dried cedar tips

½ cup (48 g) dried rosemary needles

1 cup (28 g) lavender flowers

½ cup (5 g) dried camphor southernwood leaves

½ teaspoon each cedarwood and lavender essential oils

Mixing bowl (plastic or glass)

Instructions

The Drawer Sachets

Fold fabric pieces in half with right sides together to form a 6- x 12½-inch (15- x 31.5-cm) rectangle. Sew long edges together with ½-inch (1.5-cm) seams and turn right sides out. Fold down top edge of the bag to the inside about 4 to 4½ inches (10 to 11.5 cm). Do not press; pressing leaves a mark on the fabric that will show through. You may want to tack the folded-section down lightly with a needle and thread to hold in place. If you leave it untacked, make sure the rubber band catches the edge of the fold.

Mix the herbs (cedar shavings and tips, rosemary, lavender, and camphor southernwood) and the essential oils (cedarwood and lavender) together in a nonwooden mixing bowl. Don't use a wooden spoon, either; the wood will absorb the scent. Fill the sachet with the herbal blend up to the edge of the folded-in portion of bag. Secure with a rubber band.

Wrap cording around the rubber band several times and tie in a decorative knot. Knot loose ends of cording to prevent fraying. Work with the neck of the sachet to create a full look. Makes two sachets.

The Closet Sachet

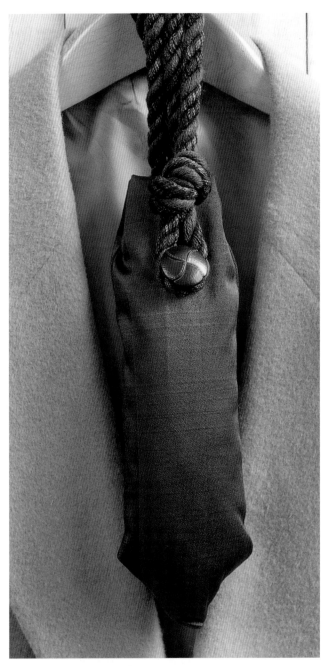

Fold the 4½- x 19-inch (11.5- x 48.5-cm) piece of fabric into a 4½- x 9½-inch (11.5- x 24-cm) rectangle, with the right sides together. Using a pen, mark a center point at the tip of the folded end of the rectangle as shown in Figure 1. Draw a diagonal line from this point to a point 2 inches (5 cm) up each side of the rectangle. Sew along these lines, then

continue to stitch up the side of the bag with a ½-inch (1.5-cm) seam. Turn the bag inside out, trim, and press. On the upper (open) end of the bag, fold down raw edges of fabric to the inside of the bag about ½ inch (1.5 cm).

Make the herbal blend as described for the drawer sachets on page 100. Fill the bag tightly with the mixture. Fold a 2-foot (.6-m) length of cording in half and knot twice as shown in Figure 2. Slip loose ends of knotted cording about ½ inch (1.5 cm) into the open end of the bag and sew straight across the top about ¼ inch (.5 cm) in from the edge. Sew button on center front of sachet, 2 inches (5 cm) down from the top edge.

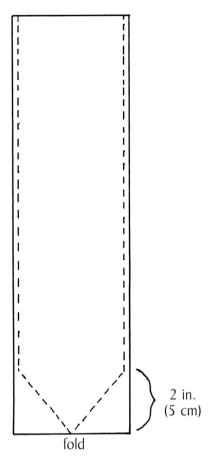

2 in. (5 cm)

fold

FIG. I

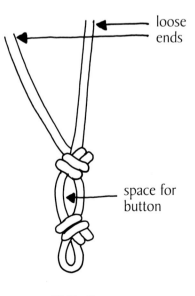

loose ends

space for button

FIG. 2

🌿 Design: Kim Tibbals-Thompson

Potpourri Bag

You Will Need

For outside of bag: 2 pieces of fabric,
7 x 8½ inches (18 x 21.5 cm)

For inside of bag: 2 pieces of fabric,
7 x 9½ inches (18 x 24 cm)

Small embroidery scissors

Cording in a coordinating color

Garden potpourri (see instructions on page 103)

Instructions

Position the two pieces of fabric for the outside bag on top of each other with right sides together. Pin and stitch the two longer sides and one short side together with a ½-inch (1.5-cm) seam. Turn right side out.

Multipurpose Scented Bags and Garden Potpourri

❦

This wonderful sewn bag design is a fabulous way to present your homemade potpourri recipe, but it can also be used as a storage or travel bag for jewelry, cosmetics, and so forth. The shoe bag (page 103) has a pouch of cedar chips attached inside. It's a nice scented gift for a man.

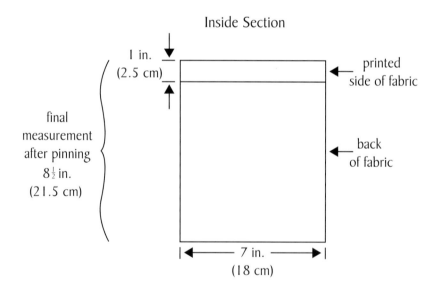

Inside Section

1 in. (2.5 cm)

printed side of fabric

back of fabric

final measurement after pinning 8½ in. (21.5 cm)

7 in. (18 cm)

Position the two pieces of fabric for the inside section with right sides together. On one short edge of each piece, fold and press 1 inch (2.5 cm) toward the wrong side as shown. This will create a finished edge when the sides are stitched and the piece is folded down. After pinning, the final measurement of this section should be 8½ inches (21.5 cm). Stitch the longer sides and the other, unfolded short side with a ½-inch (1.5-cm) seam. Do not reverse inside piece.

Insert the inside piece into the outside bag and fold top of bag (which now consists of both the inside and outside pieces) down 1½ inches (4 cm). Make eight buttonholes just large enough for the cording. Use embroidery scissors to cut buttonholes. Beginning with the middle hole in the front, thread the cording through the buttonholes. Cut cording to the desired length and tie knots at each end. Fill the bag with your favorite potpourri; this bag is filled with the garden potpourri described below.

Garden Potpourri

You Will Need

Assorted dried flowers (pansies, rose petals, statice, salvia, strawflowers, globe amaranth, and lavender)

Assorted dried herbs (scented geranium leaves, lemon verbena, and pineapple sage)

Essential oils of rose geranium and lavender

Lidded container

Instructions

For information on drying flowers and herbs, see page 18. Gently mix the dried flowers and herbs together and add drops of essential oils (rose geranium and lavender) until the desired level of fragrance is achieved. Store mixture in a lidded container, stirring twice a week. Add essential oil as needed.

 Potpourri Design: Vicki Baker

Cedar Shoe Bag

You Will Need

For outside of bag: 2 pieces of fabric, 11 x 18 inches (28 x 45.5 cm)

For inside of bag: 2 pieces of fabric, 11 x 19 inches (28 x 48.5 cm)

Small embroidery scissors

Cording in a coordinating color

Pouch of muslin filled with cedar chips

Snap

Cedar essential oil (optional)

Instructions

Follow the sewing instructions for the potpourri bag above. You will need to adjust the proportions for the larger fabric sizes, but the process is exactly the same.

To make the cedar-filled sachet for the inside of the bag, sew two squares of cotton muslin together, leaving a 2-inch (5-cm) opening. Turn the pouch inside out, fill with cedar chips, and handstitch pouch closed. Attach the cedar pouch to the inside of the inner bag with a snap. Refresh scent with cedar essential oil as desired.

 Bag Design: Mardi Letson

More Great Gifts

 Once you're
hooked on making
scented gifts,
you'll be surprised
by how many ways
you can sneak in a
little fragrance.
Here are some
imaginative gifts
that are as fun to
make as they are
to give.

Simple Sachets

Muslin tea bags (found in most heath food stores) can be purchased ready to fill with your favorite blend of dried herbs or spices. They're easily embellished with silk ribbon, stamping, and beads.

You Will Need

Reusable muslin/cheesecloth tea bags

Materials for decorating bags: premade silk-ribbon flowers (found in craft and fabric stores), millinery leaves, rubber stamp (acrylic paint or ink pad)

Materials for ties: decorative cord, assorted beads, and silk ribbon

Newsprint or cardboard

Foam or sponge applicator brush

Large-eye tapestry needle

Fine sewing needle and neutral-colored thread

Instructions

Bold Spiral Sachet

Use a premade rubber stamp or make your own rubber stamp out of self-adhesive rubber stamp material. To make your own stamp, simply cut out the shape you wish, peel off the backing, and affix backing to a small block of scrap wood.

Fold a piece of newsprint or cardboard to fit inside the tea bag; this prevents ink or paint from bleeding onto the opposite side of the bag. You can use either acrylic paint or an ink pad. If you use paint, apply it to the stamp with a foam or sponge applicator brush. Stamp your design onto the bag one side at a time. Allow the decorated side time to dry before applying the design to the other side.

When the design is dry, remove the newsprint from the inside of the bag then pull the string out of the bag casing. Thread a decorative cord through a large-eye tapestry needle and run the cord through the casing. Finish off the cord by threading decorative beads on each end. Fill the bag with potpourri or other scented materials. This designer has used a bold cinnamon blend to complement the bold design on the bag.

Delicate Floral or Leaf Sachet

Simply stitch a silk-ribbon flower or millinery leaf to the bag, using small, invisible stitches. Just a few stitches will be sufficient. Remove the string from the bag casing and thread several pieces of silk ribbon (about 7 inches or 18 cm long) through a tapestry needle. Run the ribbons through the casing. Fill either bag with a delicate scent; lavender flowers or scented geranium leaves would work well.

Design: Terry Taylor

Holiday Ornaments

Although this designer uses these sachets as Christmas ornaments (the heat from the Christmas-tree lights brings out the scent), the simple design lends itself to many decorative uses. Trimmed with greenery and tiny pine cones and placed in a bowl, they make an attractive centerpiece—and your guests can take them home at the end of the evening as party favors. They can also be attached to gift bags, packages, or wreaths, or tied along a ribbon to form a garland.

You Will Need

Fabric squares: ¼ yard (.2 m) of 45-inch (114.5 cm) fabric will make five sachets

½ yard (.45 m) of ribbon for each sachet

100% cotton ball or cotton cosmetic pad

Acrylic stuffing

Assorted spices, such as whole cloves and allspice

Pinking shears or serger

Essential oil (optional)

Instructions

Cut fabric into 7- to 9-inch (45- to 58-cm) squares. Use pinking shears or a serger to finish edges. Place spices and a 1- to 1½-inch (2.5- to 4-cm) ball of stuffing in the center of each square. If you want to use scented oil, put one or two drops on a cotton ball or cosmetic pad and place it in the center of the square along with the stuffing and the spices.

Draw up the corners and edges and tie with a ribbon. Use a hammer or your fist to crush the spices to release the fragrance. Store the sachets in a sealed plastic bag. *Caution:* scented oils sometimes remove the finish from furniture, so don't place ornaments on painted or varnished surfaces.

❦ Design: Barbara Morgan

Citronella Votives

❧❦❧

Since citronella is an insect repellent, these simple votives are a terrific gift for the friend who's glued to the deck in warm weather. Any candle scent or essential oil could be used in place of citronella.

You Will Need

2 pounds (908 g) paraffin wax with a 131° F (55° C) melting point

½ teaspoon candle dye, cut into slivers

2 teaspoons citronella candle scent or several drops citronella essential oil

2 feet (.6 m) small, metal-core candle wick

12 small metal tabs

Crock pot or double-boiler setup

Candy or wax thermometer

Pliers or tweezers

Vegetable spray

Muffin pan

Instructions

First, cover your work space with freezer paper; this will protect your work surface and make cleanup easier. You can melt the wax either in a crock pot on high or in a double boiler. Do not leave the pot unattended for any reason while the hot wax is melting! It is very important that the wax not get too hot. The flash point (point at which the wax will ignite) varies for different types of wax; make sure you know what it is for your wax before you begin. Keep a wax or candle thermometer handy and frequently check the temperature of the wax.

While the wax is melting, cut the wick into twelve 1¾-inch (4.5-cm) lengths and use tweezers or pliers to connect the wicks to metal wick tabs. Depending on the size of the muffin pan, the wick size may vary; ask your local candle or craft supply store for wicks that are suitable for your votives. Spray muffin pan well with vegetable spray.

When wax is completely melted and just before you pour the candles, stir in candle dye and citronella oil. You should pour the votives when the wax reaches 190° F (88° C). When you have reached the desired temperature, pour the wax into the spaces of a muffin tin. (You can also use a large spoon that has been bent into a ladle.) Fill each muffin cup to the top.

Press wicked tabs into the center of each cup. You may need to gently work with wicks so that each wick stands upright. Set aside to cool. As the wax cools, it will shrink and air pockets will form. You will need to top off the votives with additional wax once the wax has hardened. After the wax has cooled, place muffin pan in freezer for one hour. (This will make it easier to remove candles.) Tilt the muffin pan and carefully remove the candles. Wait 24 hours to light.

🕯 Design: Pamela Brown

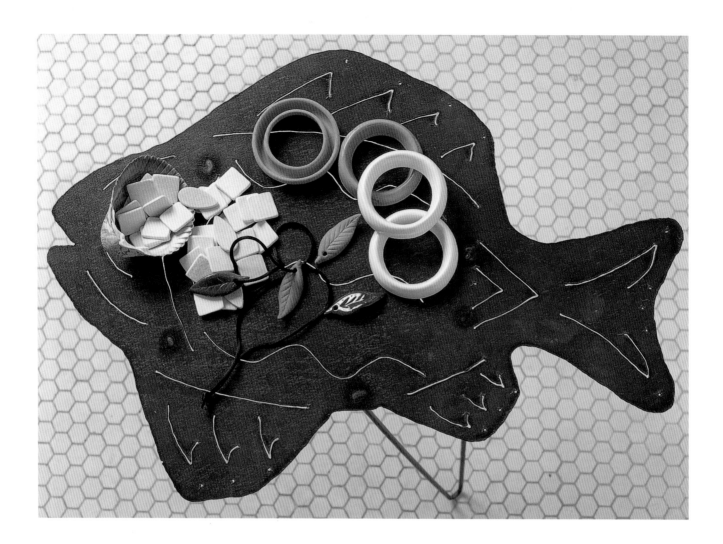

Fragrant Clay Gifts

✦✦✦

If you are itching to get your hands in clay, but don't have the money to invest in a full-scale, at-home ceramics operation, don't despair. Clay is readily available at clay or ceramics supply stores and many of these stores will fire your work for very little money. And one great thing about clay is that, when unglazed, it is porous and accepts essential oils nicely.

Here are a few simple projects that make wonderful gifts. All these can be washed by hand or in a dishwasher—so the essential oil can be changed as desired.

You Will Need

Low-fire stoneware clay; it is available either in red or white.

Assorted cutting tools

Instructions

Clay Potpourri

This project is perfect for the dried-flower-weary gift giver. In fact, this potpourri will hold its scent for a long time. To make the pieces, simply roll out clay on a piece of canvas or other textured surface, then cut the clay into pieces in any shape or size you desire. (Pieces that are longer than 1 inch [2.5 cm] can become unwieldy.) You can also roll the clay into balls, use small cookie cutters, or even shape them into flower petals to more closely imitate "real" potpourri. Take the potpourri to your local ceramics store to be fired. Once fired and just before you give the potpourri, drizzle or spray essential oil on pieces and stir gently.

Aromatherapy Lamp Rings

These popular rings are found in specialty stores but are quite easy to make. They fit directly on the light bulb; when oil is placed in the grooved area, the heat from the bulb warms the oil and diffuses it into the air.

You will need to shape the ring by hand. First, form a long, circular strip of clay that measures approximately 9½ inches (24 cm). Bend the strip around and join the edges to form a circle. The finished ring should have a 3-inch (7.5-cm) diameter at the top (where the oil will go), so add or pinch off clay as needed to achieve the correct size. Shape the clay to the approximate form shown in the photograph. The bottom side of the ring should be tapered to approximately 2½ inches (6.5 cm) to fit snugly on the light bulb. You can use a light bulb to help shape the ring, if necessary.

This designer put a clear glaze on the bottom of his rings so that the essential oils would stay on the upper surface of the ring (making it less messy). This, of course, requires purchasing a glaze and is optional. Take the aromatherapy ring to your local ceramics store to be fired. Include a bottle of essential oil when you present the gift.

Clay Charms

Body heat releases the scent from these clay charms when they are worn around the neck. There are endless possibilities with respect to design—here, we've formed leaves by hand and used a knife to make the details in the leaves. Again, one side of each of these leaves has been painted and glazed, but they work just as well unpainted and unglazed. Be sure to make a hole for the string before you take the pieces to the ceramics supply store to be fired. Once they are fired, hang the medallions on a simple black cord as shown or on any other attractive ribbon or string. Sprinkle drops of essential oil on the unglazed sides of the leaves. These charms also make great earrings, bracelets, or car ornaments.

🕯 Design: Peirce Clayton

Vintage Sachet Dolls

These dolls can be made out of almost any fabric, though vintage fabric creates an especially appealing, antique look. When using vintage materials, the design is somewhat determined by the available materials. Make sure you choose fabric that is in good shape. Don't disregard fabric that is damaged, though; you might be able to use a portion of the piece, and it will probably be less expensive than new fabric.

You Will Need

Inner pillow: cotton muslin
(18 x 12 inches or 45.5 x 30.5 cm)
or long, narrow pillowcase

Vintage table runner, vintage pillowcase, or other assorted fabric pieces

Polyester stuffing

Ribbon, 1 to 2 yards (.9 to 1.8 m)

Dried lavender and flaxseed or already-prepared sachet

Instructions

Vintage Pillowcase Doll (left)

Begin by making a narrow pillow to go inside the pillowcase. It should measure approximately 18 by 6 inches (45.5 x 15 cm). Cut a piece of muslin to this measurement, fold the fabric in half the long way, and stitch the two long sides together. Fill the inner pillow loosely with a mixture of flaxseed and dried lavender, potpourri, and polyester stuffing. Either stitch the open side closed or tie with a piece of ribbon. To stitch, turn the raw edges to the inside and hem the bottom (open end) by turning under ¼ inch (.5 cm) twice, then pressing and stitching. If you prefer to tie the opening closed, use pinking shears to finish the edges.

Center stuffed pillow inside pillowcase, pushing it to the top (closed) end of the case. Place a small amount of polyester stuffing along top seams and corners of pillowcase. Make the doll's head by pushing filler material to the top of the case and tying a ribbon bow just in from the top. Gather pillowcase 3 to 4 inches (7.5 x 10 cm) below neck to make waist. Tie in the same fashion as you did to make the head. Tie ribbon at pillowcase corners (about 1½ inches [4 cm]) to form hands.

Vintage Lace Doll (right)

Because of the chosen materials, this doll is necessarily smaller. The ecru table runner used here is approximately 38 inches (96.5 cm) long. It is lined with a muslin pillowcase, measuring 14 x 15 inches (35.5 x 38 cm). Because the doll is smaller, the long, narrow pillow is not necessary. Hands were not tied off on the vintage lace doll to give the illusion of wings. The drape on the head was made from a darker, semicircular piece of scrap lace.

Design: Barbara Morgan

Scented Journal

A journal with a handmade paper cover is the next best thing to a hand-bound book. Hand-made paper is available at craft stores or you can make your own (see page 122). Make sure you choose paper that is durable and sturdy.

You Will Need

Small journal

Cover paper

White craft glue

Small paintbrush

Ribbon

Several drops of essential oil

Rolling pin

Wax paper

Dried flowers (optional)

Instructions

Cut paper to a rectangular size that will cover the book or journal you've chosen (including spine), plus an additional 1 inch (2.5 cm) on each side. Using a fine ballpoint pen, lightly draw a straight line 1 inch (2.5 cm) in from the bottom on the underside of the paper. Make a small mark at the midpoint of this line and another mark directly above it, approximately 1 inch (2.5 cm) from the top. These marks will help you align the book on the paper.

Using the paintbrush, spread a thin, even layer of craft glue on the underside of the paper. Align the middle of the spine with the marked midpoint. Use marks to align the book in a straight line on the paper. Carefully attach the front cover, roll the book over to press the paper to the spine, then attach the paper to back cover. Use a rolling pin to smooth.

To finish corners, fold in both corners on front side as shown, then carefully fold over paper on the short side. Using scissors, make two small, straight incisions (see arrows) where the inside front cover meets the spine. The length of the incision should be just long enough to allow you to fold the bottom and top of the paper neatly over the front cover. Repeat the

above steps with the back cover. Two small tabs of paper will remain at the spine. Trim them so they can be tucked into the spine area.

Cut ribbons to the desired length and glue them in place on the inside of each cover. Glue a small piece of scrap paper over the ribbon, leaving the end of the ribbon exposed about ½ inch (1.5 cm). Turn this ½-inch (1.5-cm) piece of ribbon over on itself and glue to secure in place. Cut two pieces of paper to the exact size of the inside cover plus the front page. Spread glue on these and press paper to inside cover. Hold in place for several seconds, then use rolling pin to smooth.

Insert a piece of wax paper between the front cover and front page of book, wrap around outside and insert between back cover and last page of book. Allow to dry under pressure. This will keep the pages from sticking together as the glue dries.

Hot-glue dried flowers to cover, if desired. To scent, add a few drops of essential oil to the inside cover and keep the book closed for several days so that the scent will permeate the paper.

Design: Mardi Letson

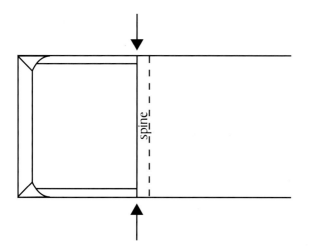

Scented Frames

A hot-glue gun, some potpourri, and a little imagination can transform
a simple picture frame into a scented treasure.

Pretty Potpourri Frame

You Will Need

Picture frame

Potpourri of your choice

Hot-glue gun

Instructions

The frame and the chosen potpourri should complement each other. Here, the designer chose a gardenia-scented potpourri and a frame with a floral design and antiqued look. The colors and shapes of the individual pieces of the potpourri and the frame work nicely together.

Pour the potpourri into a basket or onto a piece of newspaper and spend some time sorting through the pieces to get a feel for all of the elements—leaves, dried blossoms, bark peelings, and so forth. Notice the sizes, shapes, and colors. Once you have determined which pieces you want to use, lay out the pieces on the frame. Leaves and foliage make good base material, with the other, more delicate or colorful material placed on and around the leaves.

Once you are pleased with the design, hot-glue the potpourri to the frame in sections, removing only one or two pieces at a time so that you don't lose track of your design. Look for any bare spots in the design and hot-glue tiny leaves to holes.

Vanilla-Spice Frame (pictured on page 118)

You Will Need

Wooden picture frame

Cinnamon sticks

Cloves

Assorted buttons

Vanilla essential oil

Sandpaper

Serrated knife

Hot-glue gun

Instructions

Choose any wooden frame that suits you, as long as it has a flat surface. The frame will, to some extent, determine the design. First, sand the surfaces of the frame lightly so that the hot glue will attach more easily and so that the essential oil will permeate the wood. Rub the essential oil on the frame with a paper towel or rag. Be careful not to waste the oil—it is very potent and quite expensive.

Cut the cinnamon sticks to the desired length with a serrated knife. (The sticks have a tendency to crack or break when cut with scissors.) Arrange the materials—cinnamon sticks, cloves, and buttons—on the frame to determine placement. Hot-glue each item to the frame. You might want to give a bottle of vanilla essential oil with this frame, as the scent will eventually fade and the oil will need to be reapplied.

Design: Catharine Sutherland

Bay Leaf Frame

You Will Need

Wooden or plastic picture frame

Dried bay leaves

Hot-glue gun

Bay-leaf essential oil (optional)

Instructions

This is a great way to make use of an old frame that you can't bear to throw away. Since virtually all of the surface of the frame is covered, the only requirement is that the frame's surface be fairly flat. You can buy bay leaves in bulk from health food stores or gourmet supermarkets. Try to find a source that allows you to choose large, unbroken, and nicely shaped leaves. For this frame, which is 6½ x 8½ inches (16.5 x 21.5), we used about 40 leaves.

You will need to glue on two layers of leaves. Begin hot-gluing the first layer of leaves to the frame in the corners, then fill in between the corners. Make sure all the stems are pointing to the inside of the frame (or toward the photograph) and that the leaves extend beyond the edges of the frame. Use the smaller leaves and any broken ones on the first layer and the larger leaves on the second layer. Though dried bay leaves do have subtle fragrance, you will probably want to add several drops of bay-leaf essential oil for additional scent.

Design: Kelly Davis

Essential Oil Pendants

❧✦❧

Pendants made from small essential oil vials are not only attractive when worn around the neck, but they also allow the wearer to experience easily the effects of aromatherapy (see page 122).

You Will Need

Polymer clay in assorted colors

Essential oil bottles

Floral wire

Leather cording

Assorted tools for cutting

Instructions

Leafy Vine Bottle

First, roll a piece of green polymer clay into a long, thin string. This will be the vine. Cut a small piece of floral wire and bend into a small circle. Cover the wire circle with green clay to form a hanger. Place green hanger at the top of the essential oil bottle and begin green vine at the base of the hanger. Wrap the vine around the bottle, leaving space for the leaves.

Using a sharp knife, cut 15 green leaves out of green polymer clay. Place leaves on bottle: some against the vine, some separate from it, and others in small clusters. Make tiny balls from purple polymer clay and place on bottle in spots where the vine meets the leaves. Use a pencil or sculpting tool to make vein lines in the leaves. Bake bottle (without lid) for 15 minutes at 275° F (135° C). Attach cording to the hanger.

The Fading Bottle

Mix purple polymer clay with different amounts of gray polymer clay to make three or four shades of purple. Do the same with black and gray polymer clay. Roll each color into long, thin tubes. Starting with the darkest purple, wrap each tube around the bottle once and remove excess. Leave some space between each color. Cover the bottom of the bottle with black clay.

Carefully roll the bottle over a flat surface. Keep rolling until all of the lines meet each other. Make two wire loops with floral wire. Make two small balls of each basic color (purple, gray, and black) and attach the loops to the bottle with the colored balls. Form two beads out of the various colors of clay to match the bottle. Bake bottle (without lid) and beads for 15 minutes at 275° F (135° C). Thread beads on cording, then attach cording to hanger.

Pinwheel Bottle

For this bottle, you will need to make a polymer clay cane, or a log of clay with a design running through its entire length. Each slice cut from the log will show the pattern.

First, you will need to create a ½-inch (1.5-cm) cylinder as shown in the illustration. (The drawing shows the actual size of the cylinder.) Cut pieces from purple and peach polymer clay and fit them together: five triangles and a central circle (really a ½-inch-tall [1.5-cm] cylinder) from the purple clay and five rectangles from the peach clay. Place the peach pieces around the center piece as shown, then fill

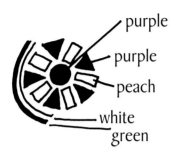

in spaces with the purple triangles. Roll out thin lengths of white and green polymer clay and cover the edges of the cylinder, first with white clay, then with green clay.

The next step is to roll the cylinder into a long tube. Be very careful, and do this very slowly. Start by gently pressing the sides and flattening the top and bottom of the cylinder. Begin to roll the cylinder on a flat surface. (You will lose some of the pattern on each end.)

For this project, the pattern will need to be different sizes, so after you have rolled for a while, cut some off. Then roll the tube thinner and cut another section off. Continue to roll and cut until you have at least five sizes of the tube. Polymer clay is much easier to cut when it is cold, so put the chunks of polymer clay in the freezer for half an hour. Once the clay has chilled, slice off pieces from each section with a sharp razor blade.

Make a loop of floral wire and wrap the wire around the neck of the bottle. Begin pressing the pieces of clay to the bottle at the bottom, beginning with the

widest slices. Leave small spaces between the slices. Continue to press slices of clay to bottle, placing increasingly small slices as you move toward the top of the bottle. Use the upper slices to cover the wire, but leave the loop uncovered. Cover the bottom of the bottle with clay last.

When the bottle is covered with slices, roll it on a flat surface until there is no more space between the slices. You will have to use your fingers to smooth the top slices over the wire. You can use the razor blade to straighten the clay at the top of the bottle.

Form beads from some of the unused slices and make holes through the centers of the beads. (The holes are much easier to make when the clay is still frozen.) Bake bottle (without lid) and beads at 275° F (135° C) for 15 minutes. Thread the beads on the cording and attach cording to the hanger.

Caution: Polymer clay is toxic. Wash your hands and work surfaces thoroughly and keep clay away from children.

 Design: Melanie Woodson

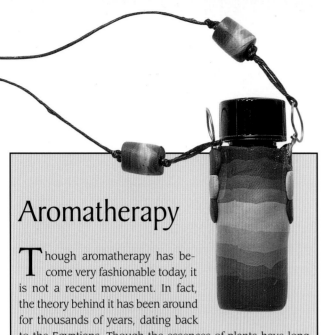

Aromatherapy

T hough aromatherapy has become very fashionable today, it is not a recent movement. In fact, the theory behind it has been around for thousands of years, dating back to the Egyptians. Though the essences of plants have long been used medicinally, the term itself was coined at the turn of the century by R. M. Gattefossé, a French scholar and chemist. Gattefossé determined that the skin and nose could help send the healing benefits of aromatic oils to other parts of the body.

In aromatherapy, essential oils, or highly concentrated oils that have been extracted from plants, are used to achieve healing and mood enhancing effects. Essential oils are quite costly, since it takes an extraordinary amount of raw material to produce a very small amount of essential oil. To make 2.5 pounds (1.1 kg) of lavender essential oil, about 440 pounds (200 kg) of fresh lavender is needed. Aromatherapists attempt to achieve very specific results by choosing essential oils that create the desired effects.

There are several methods of extracting essential oils from plants. The most common method, distillation, is a process by which steam is passed through the plant material. The steam is then collected by a special lid and sent to the coil, where the steam is condensed back to water. Because the oil is not water soluble, the oil separates from the water and is collected easily.

Essential oils can be mixed with other ingredients in cosmetics and medical preparations, inhaled into the respiratory system, or simply doused onto objects. Essential oils are very powerful and should be used sparingly. They should never be taken internally.

Scented Handmade Paper

Flower pieces give this handmade paper its appealing color and texture. It is surprisingly easy to make and the paper absorbs scents extremely well. Tie loose sheets together with a pretty ribbon or make a simple folder.

You Will Need

2 wooden picture frames, approximately the size of the paper you wish to make

Screening

Cotton, acid-free paper (high-quality watercolor paper)

Assorted flowers, with their foliage

Brown paper

Felt, cut into pieces 2 inches (5 cm) wider than the frames

2 pieces of plywood, cut at least 2 inches (5 cm) wider than the felt

Essential oil, several drops

Blender

Rolling pin

Large dishpan

Instructions

Before you begin papermaking, you will need to make a mold and deckle—these helpful tools are easily made and allow the water to drain away from the pulp (see photo on page 123). The simplest method is to use two identical wooden picture frames. First, stretch and staple a piece of screen to one picture frame to form the mold. Place duct tape around the edges of the frame to prevent pulp from being trapped in the screen edges or in the staples. The other frame will be the deckle.

Tear cotton paper into pieces and blend paper pieces with warm water in a blender to make a pulp. Set pulp aside in a bowl and continue to blend paper until you have the desired amount of pulp. The amount of paper you glean from the pulp will be approximately the amount of paper you put into it. Clean blender thoroughly. Next, blend flowers with water (again, in a blender); feel free to include stems and leaves. Blend each color of flower separately, and store in separate jars until they are needed.

Fill a dishpan about half full of warm water. Scoop some paper pulp out and put in dishpan. Stir pulp around until it is suspended in the warm water evenly. Sprinkle flower pulp into dishpan—most of the flower mixture will float on the surface. Place deckle on mold, then hold the mold and deckle in a vertical position above the dishpan and, using a continuous motion, put the mold edge into the pulp water towards the farthest side of the pan. When a horizontal position is reached, lift the mold straight up and out of the pan in a single, continuous movement.

Gently shake the mold to allow the water to drain. Let most of the water drain out of the mold and carefully remove the deckle from the mold. (If you haven't let it drain long enough, the deckle might drip onto your paper and make a hole. If this happens, immerse the pulp back in the dishpan and try again.)

Handmade molds and deckles

Once your paper is complete, you will need to couch it between pieces of felt. Position one piece of plywood on a level surface and place several sheets of brown paper on top of the plywood. Lay a piece of felt on top of the brown paper. *Note:* the brown paper should be slightly smaller than the plywood; the felt should be 2 inches (5 cm) smaller on all sides than the plywood; and the paper should be 2 inches (5 cm) smaller on all sides than the felt.

Once you have the plywood, paper, and felt in place, it is time to lay the paper on the felt. Hold the mold upright with its longest edge on the longest side of the felt and begin to gently roll the mold over onto the felt. This process is called *couching*. Place another piece of dampened felt on top of the couched sheet and carefully smooth out any wrinkles. At this point, you can make another sheet of paper and couch it directly on top of the first piece. Continue this process until you have made the desired number of pages. When you have finished couching, cover the top sheet with an extra piece of felt, then place the second plywood board on top of the stack. Apply clamps to the plywood

setup and leave for 45 minutes, tightening the clamps as much as possible every ten minutes.

While the paper is in the press, prepare your drying surface by laying wax paper out on any flat surface. Remove the clamps and carefully separate each sheet from the one below it. First, lift the felt off the stack by its diagonal corners. The paper should stay attached to the piece of felt below it. Lay the paper on the drying surface with the paper facing down and use a rolling pin to roll over the felt. Lift the felt from the back of the paper. Allow the paper to dry overnight, then peel it off the drying surface.

Bound Handmade Paper Folder

You Will Need

3 pieces of handmade paper

3 pieces of card stock, the same size as the pieces of paper

Glue stick

Twine or thick thread

Large needle

Instructions

To make a folder to hold the handmade paper, pick out three large pieces of homemade paper. One will be the front cover, one the back cover, and the other should be cut to make two pocket pieces. The pocket pieces should be slightly less than half the length and the same width as the cover pieces.

Cut pieces of thick paper or card stock to the same size as each of the four pieces (see previous paragraph). Use a glue stick to glue each piece of card stock to a matching piece of handmade paper. Make sure the most attractive sides of the handmade paper are facing outward on each piece.

Lay out the folder so that the handmade paper sides of the cover pieces are facing down and the handmade paper sides of the pockets are facing up. Using twine or thick thread, sew around the edges of the folder with a basting stitch about ¼ inch (.5 cm) from the edge. Stitch across the top of each pocket first (beginning at the outer edge), then when you get to the inside edge, turn down and stitch the pocket to the cover. Do the same with the other pocket piece.

When you have stitched both halves of the cover, lay them together, with the pockets to the inside and at the bottom of the folder. Punch three holes along the left side of the closed folder with a large needle. Thread pieces of twine through each hole and tie loosely so that the folder will open easily.

 Design: Melanie Woodson

Contributing Designers

VICKI BAKER is a horticulturist and designer who specializes in dried herbs and flowers grown on her farm, Herbworks and Everlastings, in Marshall, North Carolina. She sells her plants, bottled herb vinegars, and custom floral work at farmer's markets and craft fairs.

CATHY LYDA BARNHARDT is in charge of the floral department at Biltmore House in Asheville, North Carolina, the largest private home in North America. Her specialty is creating floral designs that concentrate on texture and depth.

ANNE BRIGHTMAN has been a floral designer and decorator for 10 years at Biltmore House and restaurants on the Biltmore Estate in Asheville, North Carolina. She was born in southern Wales and has lived in the United States since the early 1970s. She enjoys working in her garden and specializes in the English garden style of floral designs.

PAMELA BROWN is a professional candlemaker who owns and operates Mountain Lights, a candle and lighting shop in Asheville, North Carolina. In addition to her line of hand-dipped candles, she creates candleholders made from recycled products.

PEIRCE CLAYTON is a potter and business owner who lives in Minneapolis, Minnesota. His book, *The Clay Lover's Guide to Making Molds* (Lark), is due out early 1998. He designs and produces molded ceramics through his home business, Fresh Baked Studios.

NORMA CONEY is the author of *The Complete Soapmaker* (Sterling/Lark, 1996) and *The Complete Candlemaker* (Lark, 1997). She resides in Pennellville, New York, where her business, Tanglewood Gardens, is also located.

KELLY DAVIS is a product development specialist at a craft publisher and, thus, has her finger on the pulse of the craft world. She lives in Asheville, North Carolina, with her children, Bailey and Zachary.

When PATRICK DORAN is not graciously designing herb gardens for his wife's books, he spends his free time organic gardening and woodworking.

KATHLEEN GIPS owns and operates The Village Herb Shop in Chagrin Falls, Ohio. Her shop features a wide selection of herbal products for home and family and specializes in tussie-mussies, posy pins, and herb seasoning mixes.

BETH HERDMEN is a soapmaker, a dried herbal crafter, and a potter. She and her husband own and operate a small organic vegetable farm, Dancing Woods Farm, in Mars Hill, North Carolina. She has three girls.

KIRSTEN JASNA works in fund-raising in Minneapolis, Minnesota. She enjoys crafting (especially with buttons), gardening, and spending time with her dogs.

CASEY KELLAR lives in Scappoose, Oregon. She is the owner of RainCountry Naturals and RainShadow Labs, which formulate and manufacturer all-natural bath, beauty, and home fragrance products. She is also the author of *The Natural Beauty and Bath Book* (Lark, 1997).

Contributing Designers (cont.)

CORKY KURZMANN works to teach children in her community through educational craft projects. Known for her high energy level, Corky spends her free time gardening, canning, preserving, and herbal crafting.

MARDI LETSON is a social worker who lives in Asheville, North Carolina, with her husband, Kellett, and her dogs, Moses and Shelby. She creates gorgeous floral crafts and home decorative items in her basement studio.

BARBARA MORGAN is an widely exhibited artist who specializes in hand-colored photographs. She lives in Birmingham, Alabama, and is a faculty member of the University of Alabama.

TRACY MUNN is a sewing dynamo who recently built a separate barn to house her many fabrics and supplies. She had a dressmaking business in South Carolina, before moving to Asheville, North Carolina, in 1995. She loves making clothes for her family and home decorating items for her bungalow in the country.

ALYCE NADEAU lives in Lansing, North Carolina, and is the author of *Making and Selling Herbal Crafts* (Sterling/Lark, 1995). Past president of the North Carolina Herb Association, Alyce conducts herb classes, creates herbal weddings, and markets her handcrafted herbal creations at farmer's markets, juried craft shows, and through her business, Goldenrod Mountain Herbs.

SHERRI SATTERWHITE is an assistant editor for a technical publication, but plans to go back to business school. She spends her free time gardening at her home in Apex, North Carolina.

GEORGIA SHUFORD is widely recognized for her expert culinary skills. She lives in Marion, North Carolina with her dachshund companion, Little John.

CATHARINE SUTHERLAND is a student at the University of North Carolina at Asheville, where she majors in English Literature. She hopes to pursue a career in publishing when she graduates. Most recently, she was an indispensable editorial intern for Lark Books.

TERRY TAYLOR specializes in creating art for the garden using pique-assiette, or shard art, technique. Terry is known for his willingness to try any craft—and does a fabulous job at whatever he tries. He collects, creates, and carves from his home in Asheville, North Carolina.

KIM TIBBALS-THOMPSON resides in Waynesville, North Carolina. She is a frequent contributor to craft books and enjoys drawing, sewing, gardening, herbal crafting, and broom making. By day, she is a graphic designer.

MELANIE WOODSON lives in Asheville, North Carolina, where she is a whiz crafter. Mosaics, polymer clay, painting, beadwork, needlepoint, knitting, metalwork, and stained glass are only a few of her many talents. When she's not creating something beautiful, she sings in a band.

Project Index

Project Index (cont.)

Subject Index